Tyndale House Publishers, Inc.
Carol Stream, Illinois

LIFE
SAVRS
for WOMEN

JAMES STUART BELL
JEANETTE GARDNER LITTLETON

Visit Tyndale's exciting Web site at www.tyndale.com

TYNDALE and Tyndale's quill logo are registered trademarks of Tyndale House Publishers, Inc.

Life Savors for Women

Designed by Jacqueline L. Nuñez

Edited by Joan Hutcheson

Library of Congress Cataloging-in-Publication

Life savors for women / [compiled by] James Stuart Bell and Jeanette Gardner Littleton.
    p. cm.
  ISBN-13: 978-1-4143-1735-9 (sc)
  ISBN-10: 1-4143-1735-2 (sc)
  1. Christian women—Religious life—Anecdotes. I. Bell, James Stuart.
II. Littleton, Jeanette Gardner.
  BV4527.L53 2008
  242'.643—dc22   2007050823

Printed in the United States of America

14   13   12   11   10   09   08
7   6   5   4   3   2   1

Dedication

To Margaret, the one who walks the journey
with me and keeps me from faltering.
—James Stuart Bell

To some of the special women who've helped me savor life:
Rhonda Stock, Janie Hansen, Sally Whittaker, Vidy Metsker,
Sandy Parker, Mary Ann Cornelius, Patty Gardner,
Nicole Hooper, Alisha Littleton, and Jennifer Ferranti.
—Jeanette Gardner Littleton

CONTENTS

INTRODUCTION

When women get together, a special synergy and camaraderie occur.

This woman-bonding thing is not new. In biblical cultures, women often did their chores and marketing together. The older women taught the younger women in matters of home logistics, relationships, and godliness.

These gender connections are not limited to biblical days, either. Throughout history, in various cultures, women have given one another help, support, advice, and wisdom. Women tend to be relational creatures, and the presence of other women in our lives is often the blessed gift through which God reveals his love and grace.

That's the premise for this book. It's chick-thick with personal stories and lessons that will minister from the heart of the woman writing to the soul of the woman reading.

As you read through this book, we suspect you'll find challenge, hope, and even some heart-tugging messages that God has waiting just for you. You'll find plenty of smiles and encouragement—flavored with love and served with plenty of inspiration.

So come on in. Spend some time with three dozen favorite or new girlfriends. Let their words help you savor the full flavor of your life!

FAME REDEFINED

My acting debut and my final curtain call happened on the same day—a day that broke the needle on the Richter scale for humiliation.

I've learned a great deal from that day.

What was I thinking when I accepted the leading role of Mary in the church's annual Easter drama? Nothing, actually. I blurted out an acceptance with no thought whatsoever. After all, what was there to ponder? It was about time someone noticed my talent and beauty, not to mention my charismatic persona. *Move over, Julia Roberts—here I come!*

Unbeknownst to me, I'd been chosen because in the middle of blue-eyed, blonde, Midwestern suburbia, I had the longest brown hair and darkest eyes for a Hebrew-looking Mary. I didn't have a Jewish bone in my body. I'd never even eaten a latke, I couldn't pronounce *chutzpah,* and what exactly is a lox?

In a flattered-but-ignorant state of mind, I began to weave play practice into my already busy life filled with four children, a husband, and a dog. Homeschooling; carpooling; committee meetings; and, much to my shame, Bible study got shoved to the back burner. My inner wannabe-actress emerged with a vengeance, kind of like an out-of-control cold sore. Latent Hollywood aspirations surfaced, morphing my life into an insane sitcom—or if you asked my family, a horror movie.

Script memorization cheat sheets decorated my kitchen cupboards and bathroom mirror. I squeezed in costume fittings, leaving behind dirty dishes and a filled laundry tub. I got odd looks as I zipped to and from church in the car dressed as though I should be astride a camel instead of in a beat-up minivan. I won't even discuss the cumulative effect of four solid weeks of frozen pizza on one's digestive system. Yes, the dog's, too.

Thankfully, the big day arrived. I'd done it all, from learning stage right and stage left to gracefully maneuvering in a floor-length, first-century costume reproduction. I couldn't have been more ready—nor could my family.

Suits and new spring dresses filled the lily-perfumed sanctuary. I knew that this was a once-a-year pilgrimage to church for many people. This would be my chance to rise above my mundane Mommy life and perhaps do something really wonderful for God, something significant to further his Kingdom. In the moments before curtain call, I prayed that he'd use my performance to change hearts.

With a deep breath and a smile, I stepped onto the stage—front and center—facing a captive and expectant crowd. I would proclaim the most joyous words ever uttered to humankind. I would announce that glorious phrase offered up by Mary on the first Easter morning. I would say . . .

Now, what were those words?

Hundreds of eyes gaped at me in silence, inducing a tremor of terror that rippled through every muscle. This went way beyond knocking knees. I'm pretty sure I could feel my spleen quiver.

Fear has a way of reaching deep down and hitting one where it hurts the most—the bladder. But a restroom had nothing to do with the Good News I should've been declaring.

The metallic taste of stomach acid gurgled at the back of my throat, but other than that, nothing came out. No words. Nothing. Acute unease and sympathy pulsated in the quiet as I stood speechless on stage. How could I possibly have forgotten "He is risen!"?

What to do?

I babbled.

I babbled my way off that stage as fast as I could, scooted out a rear janitor's entrance, and fled to my car. The embarrassment that burned my cheeks and twisted my tummy rivaled a pants-wetting incident in fourth grade. And if I'd never forgotten that, how would I ever show my face in public again after this—especially at church?

The answer didn't come right away—no lightning bolts of insight or anything. I slunk home, and I stayed there. In slow motion, my thoughts kept rewinding and playing the Grand Debacle, as I had dubbed my horrible performance. Hiding in my house gave me plenty of time to think and to meditate on the lines I'd momentarily forgotten. As I began to take my focus off my failure and replace it with God's Word, something amazing happened.

Though I'd intended a sweet performance that would change hearts that Easter morning, my own heart was now being transformed. I'd wanted to do something wonderful for God. Instead, and in spite of the weeks I'd neglected my family, he did something wonderful for me: He allowed me to fail, to experience humiliation pressing down on my gut until I squirmed, to deal with the shame that burned along every exposed nerve of my body. See, God knew what I felt that Sunday morning—humiliated and ashamed. He felt it two thousand years before, hanging on a cross . . . half-naked . . . all eyes on him . . . watching . . . waiting for something to happen.

But he didn't babble and run away.

He remembered his lines. And it's his words that bring the most hope and promise: "It is finished!" (John 19:30; Revelation 21:6). Jesus took care of everything that day. Every one of my failures, my shortcomings, my major-league embarrassments went to the grave with him and were buried because of the price he paid. It's because of his victory, his resurrection, that I could let go of my pride and my striving to put on a good presentation. He lifted my head so that I wasn't afraid to show my face at church again.

Whenever I'm tempted to be ashamed, instead of viewing my past parade of flaming failures, I remember what the Good News is all about. I choose to focus on God and what he's doing in the world rather than on my own inadequacies. I think of Paul's words, "I am not ashamed of this Good News about Christ. It is the power of God at work, saving everyone who believes" (Romans 1:16). That sure takes the pressure off me and lets God's strong character shoulder the weight of my blunders. It's not up to me to save the world. But it is up to me to point to the One who can—even if I occasionally mess up and the right word combinations don't flow from my lips.

Keeping all this in the front of my mind made it easier to bear the sympathetic glances and the "it's OK" pep talks I received at church the next week. I even heard about some spectacular onstage faux pas committed by others in their past. It seems there's quite a need for a support group for those scarred by theatrical bungling.

I guess I wasn't meant to be an actress after all. The spotlight has a tendency to make me look five pounds heavier, anyway. Besides that, if I ever serve another frozen pizza at home, my family has threatened to wing it at me with the express intent of decapitation.

When the next church drama rolls around, I'll make sure to be there—smiling in the audience. Though my name's been left in the member registry, I don't think the casting director has it on his list.

Hey, Julia Roberts, don't worry. You'll be getting no competition from this girl.

—Michelle Griep

LOVED FOR MY SOUL

Have you ever wanted to be loved just for your soul? That notion and craving began to gnaw at me as I entered my mid-forties. I had been married for nearly twenty years to my best friend when I began to hunger secretly for heart-satisfying words such as "I love you for your soul."

· Such words would surpass any previous compliment. I felt that they would complete me and further seal our relationship. This thought had previously surfaced only a few times a year. However, I was suddenly overcome several times a day with the thought that I had never heard such words from anyone in my lifetime. I longed to be desired for my innermost being. So I decided to pray about this for several days.

The next week our family was vacationing where, supposedly, dreams come true, when spiritual warfare began unexpectedly, although I did not immediately recognize it as such—surely that wasn't happening to me!

We went to the pool, but I was the only one in our family who did not wear a swimsuit. I was dressed in black jeans and a sleeveless turquoise turtleneck. Shades concealed my best physical feature—my eyes. Even though it was a heated pool, the water was still too cold for this Southern girl. My husband, Ed, began playing with our three kids in the water. I was enjoying watching.

Ed is an involved father and husband, and I've never wanted to be with anyone else. I guess my private longing was just a need to be wanted in a deeper spiritual sense.

As I watched from my lounge chair and wrote in the journal I'd taken to the pool with me, I felt a piercing stare. I looked around and spotted another vacationing dad in the pool with his two kids. I repeatedly sensed his penetrating and intrusive glances at me—even up-and-down looks—as he clearly checked out my full figure.

And the smiles he flashed at me—I looked to my left, my right, and behind me to be sure. No, no one else was around. I thought, *He's got to be kidding. . . . I must remind him of someone else or maybe he's in the water without his contacts!*

Because it began to sprinkle, I moved to the shelter of an umbrella that was practically half a football field away.

Another stranger near me began polite, casual conversation. When he asked a question, I thought it would be rude not to answer so I responded briefly. In the meantime, another man in maybe his late thirties came to my table and proceeded to put down his towels, watch, and other items. I was busy writing in my journal and honestly had not noticed him until the stranger near me said, "Your husband is a really big guy."

I felt a bit puzzled because my husband is only about five feet ten with a medium build, but I proudly beamed, "Yes! He really does have great, broad shoulders."

Then the man said, "He seems to be going kind of bald. You must be so used to looking at all his muscles that you hardly notice."

By this point I'm sure I was frowning and told him, "My husband has a head full of gorgeous black hair."

The stranger pointed to the man who'd dropped his stuff at my table, who could have been a former Mr. Universe. It took all the modesty my mother raised me with to keep my jaw from dropping and my face from blushing.

Some time later "Mr. Universe" returned to pick up his items and made a big deal of drying off in front of me, flexing his pectorals. I ignored his flash of flesh and his revealing conversation: "I'm sorry for leaving all my stuff here. I'm divorced, and I'll be here with my son until Wednesday. How long will you be here?"

I motioned to my children and husband, stressing with a panicked smile, "The five of us will be going home soon!" Then I got up nervously and walked to my husband.

In waist-high water, hubby Ed began strutting like a puff-chested, feather-ruffled rooster, pretending to dry off with flexed pecs and bodybuilder poses. He had seen the display. I admit I was concerned. I think the guys were checking out "former Mr. Universe" more than I was. And it was one of the few times I had ever seen my husband act jealous. It was definitely the most animated display of envy I've seen. And he didn't care if everyone else saw it, either! Yes, this is another quality I sometimes love about him.

Ed and the stranger had noticed the muscles and the fact that he was flirting with me more than I had. Because it was foreign to me, I had not recognized it for what it really was. I thought it was just testosterone in the air.

When the coast was clear, I returned to my haven under the umbrella. The stranger asked, "So how long have you been married?"

I answered distinctly, "About twenty years."

He asked, "About a year to this guy?"

"Nearly twenty years to the same man," I emphasized. Then my heart sank as he replied, disappointed, "I've been divorced for some time now. I bring my daughter here once a month. But she does not like to ride my motorcycle with me. It's a Harley."

Finally, there was a change of subject! We had just gone into a Harley shop that morning, which was out of character for us—especially for me. I told him my husband and I had daydreamed about retirement there! I quipped, "For fun we had our kids take a picture of the two of us wearing shades 'riding' a Harley together. I'm really cautious, so that's as close to riding a Harley as I'll ever get. It must be fun to feel uninhibited enough to ride a motorcycle and not worry about it."

Ed came up to tell me he was leaving and to ask me to stay with the kids. He kissed me firmly on the lips. I did not say another word to the stranger, who left soon with his own youngster. About fifteen minutes later, the stranger suddenly reappeared, speaking with a hint of a hiss, "I really enjoyed talking with you. I don't know your name. I'm ssstaying in room number twenty-three, and later tonight you could come by for a few drinksss if you'd like a break."

I was in ssshock. Actually, disbelief! After a few ssstammers, I managed to say, "Thank you. We appreciate it, but I think my husband has plans for us."

Then I moved closer to the pool's edge. I felt like jumping in with a plea, "Lord, cleanse my soul!" The stranger slithered away.

I considered leaving a Bible verse taped to his door. But instead I decided just to silently pray for the lisping stranger.

I also decided not to tell Ed about the whole ordeal, thinking that it would hurt him and maybe even make him distrust me. However, I admit that I was flattered. I also knew I would never donate my sleeveless turquoise turtleneck when I cleaned out the closet. It would bring a smile to my face years from now when I wore it with arms that jiggled even more, along with some gravity lines. I might even have to be buried in it.

Hours later, as we left our condo for dinner, I saw the stranger emerge in the distance, hands on hips as if he had been waiting. I glanced at him for a brief, awkward second. Then I turned my back and walked away. I would not encourage him whatsoever.

I felt something dark around me. As I walked away, I realized the devil literally wanted me for my soul. I was rattled. I was not hungry for dinner, but I was starving for God's Word and time alone to pray.

No one had any idea of what was going on inside me. I silently prayed, *Lord, please secure my soul and let me hunger only for your Word. May my husband and I grow to love you more, because you have blessed our spirits with faithfulness through the sacrament of marriage.*

I wondered . . . maybe this craving I had could be satisfied only through more intimacy with Christ. After all, he is the One who should love me for my soul. Maybe the only one.

The next day was our last, and with gusto, we visited a theme park. When we left for lunch, we walked out with an elderly couple in their late seventies who were being congratulated by staffers for being married fifty-eight years. Each time someone congratulated them, the wife added, "Fifty-eight *happy* years!"

What a message of hope and light this was in my private battle with darkness during my need to be desired in a deeper way!

One evening, my husband and I were in one of those loving moods. He whispered all the sweet things this woman loves to hear from him such as, "You are my only." "You make me feel young again." "You are so beautiful." "I love you. . . . I love your soul."

My heart raced. I could not believe my ears. And I kissed him like I never had before. God had in his own way been answering my prayers all along.

—Lisa Plowman Dolensky

MY MEDAL OF HONOR

I have never fought a military battle. I have never led soldiers through land mines or enemy-held jungles. I have never risked my life in the line of duty while serving my country. Yet I feel I have received the Medal of Honor.

My call to serve began when I looked into the brown eyes of the seven-year-old boy who had come to spend a year with Dad, Mom, and me. I was twenty-eight and had never been married. My parents were in their sixties. They became Grandma and Grandpa, and I took on the role of a single mother, for which I was sadly unprepared.

That year stretched into two, three, then ten years. During those years, Justin and I were in training for the greatest battle of all—life. How many soldiers can claim ten years devoted to learning how to live, how to discipline and be disciplined? It did not come easy; it had to be understood and practiced.

Our first major skirmish arrived in the heart of winter: a season of icy roads, icicle-laden branches, and mounds of glorious snow for a boy to play in. Our steep-pitched roof was covered with aluminum. Justin delighted in climbing to the peak, spread-eagling his arms and legs, and sliding into the waiting drifts below the eaves.

Just outside our living room window, a myriad of icicles reached from the roof to the ground. The granddaddy of them all was two feet across the base and ten feet long. When Justin asked if he could break it off, I answered, "No! It could smash the window or, even worse, fall on you."

Nevertheless, one morning after breakfast a loud crash and a sudden blast of subzero air drew us to the living room. Justin stood on the snowdrifts, peering in through the smashed window. The great column of frozen crystal had been irresistible.

We covered the window with cardboard until we could get to town for replacement glass—paid for with nickels and dimes and pennies from Justin's piggy bank. It was harder for me to see Justin counting out his savings than it was for him, but as good soldiers learn from their mistakes, so did he. He knew he was paying for his disobedience as well as paying for the glass.

Later that winter, Justin disappeared. We had a standing order that he was never to leave the yard without telling us for his protection: The river was a mile away. Great stands of timber stood between our home and our neighbors. A frozen pond lay farther down the road. All these called to a boy. All were dangerous. But luckily, I had seen Justin turning into a neighbor's driveway a quarter of a mile away. He returned an hour later, stamping snow and pretending he had been in our yard all along.

One of the hardest things I ever had to say was, "Sorry! You just traded your roller-skating night for this afternoon's little jaunt."

He didn't say a word, even though the trip to the rink fifty miles away had been planned for months. For the rest of the week, he was a model child. By Friday afternoon I wished I could relent but knew Justin had to learn.

When I got ready to leave on my journey—without the side trip to the rink—he kissed me good-bye and said, "Have a good time." As he went back to reading his book in the big armchair, I knew I wouldn't have a good time. Mom later noticed his book was upside down. She turned it over. Justin was fast asleep behind the tear-spotted pages. It was a hard lesson for both of us, but Justin never again left the yard without telling us where he was going.

As he grew, Justin began making his own contributions. He sometimes showed strength when I was weak. The night before my younger brother, Randy, left for naval officer training during a time of world tension and unrest, Mom made his favorite dinner. We all pretended to eat; then Randy said, "Well, I guess it will be a while before we're all here together again."

Dad burst into tears and left the table.

We were stunned. We had never seen Dad cry.

Justin quietly slipped into the living room. We heard him say, "Don't cry, Grandpa. You've still got me."

We all cried—and felt better.

Time passed. Marbles gave way to bicycles, to barefoot-in-the-mud excursions, and to tag football. A few years later, Dad died. Strong in our belief of immortality and hope, and not wanting our final good-byes to be harder than necessary, we chose to have a simple graveside service. This broke the town tradition of holding an elaborate funeral followed by a potluck dinner for the neighbors. One lady commented, "They must not have thought much of Bill not to even have a proper funeral."

Justin overheard her. "You don't understand," he earnestly said. "That's not Grandpa, just his old house. He's been sick and his body wasn't good anymore, so he left it and moved out. It's like when an old house has broken windows and no paint. People move away and leave it."

For once, the village gossip was silenced.

Dad's death began a new era. After two cold winters without Dad's guiding hand, Mom, Justin, and I moved to a larger town. Our household seemed strange to many. But when asked if we had a generation gap, Justin replied, "Maybe. Granny doesn't climb trees, and I don't go to her senior meetings."

I found it harder to adjust than either Mom or Justin did. With Dad gone, I was head of the household, a single foster mother, and a full-time worker. I often felt harassed, worried, and resentful. Even as famous generals have spent sleepless nights pondering campaigns, I sometimes lay awake in tears, asking for strength. What did I know of a teenage boy's problems? Only by God's grace did we survive.

Heartaches followed. I spent tense hours waiting for Justin to come home, feeling fear, anger, concern, relief. There were phone calls: flat tires, broken-down cars, rides home from his evening shift at a fast-food place. Sometimes I simply donned bathrobe, slippers, and a coat to go get Justin.

Worst of all were the injuries! Cut feet, infected toes, a punctured eardrum—on and on, until the day I stood beside a hospital bed, where Justin lay suffering from broken teeth, a lacerated mouth, and a broken jaw incurred in an auto accident.

As I waited for the doctor, I pictured again the little boy from so many years before. And for the first time, I realized the depth of meaning used in bestowing the Medal of Honor: "Service above and beyond the call of duty."

Great deeds can be performed in the name of duty, but we can raise a child only with boundless love and faith in God. All the books in the world cannot equip anyone—especially a single mother—to bear the heartache, tears, and anxiety, even when they are sprinkled with joy. Or, when it's time to let go, to feel it has been worth all the struggle.

The early days are gone forever—the time we spent learning and growing, laughing and crying together. Justin has passed on, but before he left us he said, "The years I spent with you, Grandpa, and Grandma were the best times in my life."

Justin's tribute is my reward, my Medal of Honor.

—Colleen L. Reece

I hated to work puzzles, yet I was impatiently waiting in line at the store to pay for a thousand-piece jigsaw puzzle.

As a kindergarten teacher, I had the opportunity to put a lot of puzzles together, as my little five-year-olds inevitably dropped one on the floor at least once a day. As the pieces lay on the floor, they would yell, "Ms. Spivey, don't worry—I'll put it together. I know you don't do it so good!"

Sadly, they were right. A simple ten-piece puzzle could stump me until lunchtime, so why did I feel the need for a thousand-piece one? Because a little voice inside my head had been bugging me for a month to purchase one. But I could reassure myself that I had done dumber things in my life.

I set up a card table in front of the fireplace in my den, an excellent place to create my masterpiece. I sat down, opened the box, and stared at the many pieces.

Where do I start? There were so many pieces, and I didn't expect them to be so tiny. I had always told my little ones at school to start with the edge pieces, so that's what I did. There's nothing like following your own advice.

After about a week, I had the edge pieces together. Yes, it took me that long, but I was really getting into this project. Sitting in front of the fire, feeling a quiet victory each time two pieces joined, was therapeutic. My little ones at school would be proud!

My friends became a part of the process too. They would get comfortable and spend an hour or two visiting while challenging their puzzle skills. Every time they dropped by to see me, they'd head to the puzzle table. What fun this turned out to be!

In retrospect, this thousand-piece project turned out to be more than just fun. God used the puzzle to work in my love life!

Several years earlier, I had experienced a difficult, sad divorce. More than anything, I wanted a partner again, someone to love and care for. I was lonely and felt that the gaping hole in my heart could be filled only by a special man.

At the time, I was dating a good man who seemed to be "the one." He was attractive, bright, sensitive, and honest, and he dressed well and owned a beautiful home.

The only thing was, I wasn't sure he truly loved me. And when I was honest with myself, I didn't feel sparks for him, either. I kept thinking love would grow. I kept trying to make it work.

My friends told me I was trying too hard.

"This isn't love," they would say. "You shouldn't have to try so hard to make the feelings come."

I didn't believe them. They meant well, but what did they know? They had never experienced being alone in the world at age fifty-five. Being alone was not easy, so I desperately wanted this relationship to work. I prayed about it frequently and asked God to show me what to do. Should I continue with this relationship and make it work, or let it go?

One day as I worked on my puzzle, I eyed two pieces

that looked like a perfect fit. Their shapes and colors appeared compatible. I quickly picked up the pieces and shoved them together. To my surprise, they just didn't fit. I tried turning the pieces and pushing them together another way. I even wondered if the factory had failed to punch out one piece correctly. I considered shaving a little bit of it off with a knife.

As I struggled with those two pieces, I heard a voice say, *Two good pieces that just don't fit.*

I even started to mumble it to myself. "They're two good pieces that just don't fit."

All of a sudden it hit me! Wow! Jim, the fellow whom I wanted to be "the one," and I were like the puzzle pieces. We were two good people who just didn't fit. We didn't belong together any more than those two puzzle pieces belonged together.

There was nothing wrong with either of us—our Maker had created us exactly as he wanted us to be. However, he did not create us to interlock in a permanent relationship. No matter how long I tried to fit us together and make our relationship work, it simply wasn't going to. God had created each of us to fit with someone else. I wasn't sure who that "someone else" was for me, but I knew we would fit perfectly and easily.

In the middle of my den, I got down on my knees and thanked the Lord for this message of love. He didn't want me to struggle anymore with this relationship or wonder why it wasn't working. He wanted me to let go and know that he had it all under control—he had the puzzle all figured out.

I can't help but marvel at how God sends us messages and talks to us. He didn't speak to me during my quiet prayer time or even through a good friend or counselor. He spoke to me through cardboard puzzle pieces. He put in me a desire to do something I normally hate to do. That in itself got my attention. It made me focus more attentively on the experience and wonder about its importance.

Well, I let go of the relationship. I knew I was doing the right thing and had no regrets. It was difficult, but God's sweet message allowed me to let go gently, knowing I don't want anything less than the perfect fit.

God speaks to us in many ways. He is inventive and thinks outside the box! When we're struggling with a problem and we commit it to the Lord, we can keep our eyes open. We might be surprised at how the answer comes and where it comes from.

After all, who would have expected guidance through a thousand-piece jigsaw puzzle?

—Ellie Ray

HANNAH'S LEGACY

Every time I climbed the steps to begin my day of work, a feeling of awe overwhelmed me. Being the director of education at a home for unwed mothers, housed in the massive architectural wonder of a former convent, had its share of paradoxes. Having toured Italy, I wondered how the priests from previous centuries who had constructed the original Italian cathedral would have felt about having a sister church built in urban Kansas City, Missouri, to house pregnant teenagers.

Just as this beautiful old convent and house of worship had a history, the residents who now came through its doors seeking safe haven also had a past. By the time I had served these mothers-to-be for a year, I had learned that because I was no older than many of the young women I taught, my best teaching method was to really know the residents individually. Having no children of my own yet, I had time to interact with many of the young women, not only in group counseling but also outside of classes when I was no longer on duty. It was my privilege to listen to the girls' life stories, hopes, and dreams.

Because my life intersected with theirs in a time of crisis and because they lived where I worked, I became close, personal friends with a few of the young women. One of those friendships impacted me especially because her life choices were so poignant.

When I first saw Betsy across the width of the dining hall, several impressions struck me. First of all, she didn't fit the stereotype of an unwed mother. She looked mature, well groomed, and poised. She also had the demeanor of someone who camefrom a background of wealth and privilege. As I approached to greet her and introduce myself, all those qualities were confirmed. I found Betsy to be highly educated, intelligent, eloquent, and charming. Yet, I sensed sadness and pain in her eyes.

During hours of conversation over the next few months, the mystery unraveled. Betsy had indeed come from an upper-class home. She had been a sophomore at an Ivy League school, where she met Sal from Iran. This charismatic young Moslem had captivated her. She discovered that his father was a wealthy, powerful, and prominent Islamic leader. Because strict and loveless Protestant parents had raised Betsy, she was fascinated by Sal's obsessive attention toward her and was influenced by his passionate beliefs.

However, as their relationship progressed, Betsy realized how entrapped she had become. When she learned she was pregnant, Sal began to reveal a violent and possessive nature. His family pressured them to move to Iran, where Betsy would be at their mercy. Betsy began to fear for her life and that of her unborn child. She was too humiliated to ask for help from her former friends and estranged family, but when she heard about the home for unwed mothers in Kansas City, she fled to it.

Once Betsy felt safe, she embraced her Christian roots in a fresh way. She and I had lengthy discussions about philosophy and theology, concentrating on the love, mercy, and forgiveness of our heavenly Father. She began to heal as she opened her heart to receive these precious gifts from God. By the time she reached her eighth month of pregnancy, her face glowed—not only with motherhood but also with an inner peace and joy.

One day about two weeks before Betsy's due date, she and I shopped together at a Christian bookstore. We were looking at wall hangings when I heard her gasp. She held out a framed portion of Scripture for me to read. The printed verses were from 1 Samuel 1:27-28: "I asked the LORD to give me this boy, and he has granted my request. Now I am giving him to the LORD, and he will belong to the LORD his whole life."

Betsy and I had talked about this Bible story many times because it meant so much to her. This book of Samuel tells about a woman named Hannah, who had been married for years but could not have a child. She went to the Temple and wept and prayed for God to give her a son. She told God that if he granted her a child, she would offer the child back to him. God heard and answered her prayer. Hannah gave birth to a son named Samuel. When Samuel was still a small child, Hannah took him to serve God in the Temple. Samuel became one of Israel's greatest priests and prophets. He was faithful to God all of his days.

As I read the framed verses, I could not hold back the tears. Betsy had decided to give her baby up for adoption—to give her child to the Lord. I never understood why it seemed that all the girls who seemed immature and the least likely to care for their babies kept their babies, while the young women like Betsy, who could provide for their babies financially and emotionally, opted for adoption.

I did know, without a doubt, that Betsy was sacrificing what she wanted for her baby's good. She wanted her baby to have a mom and a dad. She also wanted to protect her baby from the biological father. In her mind and heart, she was giving her child to God.

Days after our shopping trip, we met again in Betsy's hospital room. I handed her the framed verses from 1 Samuel that I had brought as a gift, and she handed me her newborn baby. Betsy's daughter was adorned in an exquisitely ornate pink dress.

"Her name is Hannah," announced Betsy.

As I sat in the corner and rocked Hannah, I prayed that God would bless her and honor her as he had her namesake. Hannah of Old Testament fame had left a legacy of love, obedience, and sacrifice.

Three weeks later, the bells of the old convent pealed in honor of Hannah's adoption. I was privileged to be a part of the ceremony and to meet Hannah's wonderful adoptive parents. There were many tears and prayers over Hannah in that chapel, but I knew that God was already at work. He had promises and a plan for this new little Hannah. He would be faithful to her, and to Betsy, all of their days.

—Evangeline Beals Gardner

THE LADY AND THE TEACUP

I looked twice at the old, beat-up car. It had caught my attention while I waited at the stoplight on my way to work.

The car's lack of a good muffler caused my car windows to rattle. The tires had no hubcaps, and smoke billowed out the back of the rusted old Ford "tank."

But what really made me do a double take was the massive car's driver. To my astonishment, she was a small-framed woman wearing a scarf over her graying hair, singing to the radio while sipping from a china teacup. Yes—a china teacup.

The lovely cup was cream colored with a graceful swirl of yellow flowers winding around it. The driver didn't appear to have the saucer—just the cup. As the traffic light turned green, she took off without a care as she continued sipping with pinkie finger extended.

I was surprised to see the delicate cup because I am a teacup collector and would never dream of using mine in such a manner. I still have the cup that started my collection more than twenty-five years ago. A special shelf holds the wafer-thin cup and saucer I purchased when I was on a trip to England. One of my favorites is a colorful creation I carefully protected all the way back from Israel. The pieces of my collection are as different from one another as Goldilocks and the Three Bears—I have big ones, short ones, little ones, and broken ones. My prize collection represents every color of the rainbow, and then some.

My mom knows my love of pretty teacups, so she gave me the one I treasure most. The chalk-white cup is covered with dainty blue flowers and has a rim of gold. I keep it safe in a place of honor in my cabinet. I take it down from time to time when I need a little something special. I imagine my mother's hugs while I sip my favorite tea blend.

That evening after work, I faced a perfect occasion to relax with my favorite teacup, as well as my thoughts. As I mulled over what I had witnessed that morning, sentimental tears filled my eyes. You see, my treasured cups see hot tea only on special occasions, yet this mystery woman was sipping from a treasure while probably heading to the neighborhood Wal-Mart.

To resolve all of life's perplexing issues, I take everything to God—and I do mean everything. It may seem silly to pray about issues as small as teacups, but nothing is too small for God.

As I talked to God, I wondered why I cherished each of my teacups so much. The answer was fairly easy—each of them represents a trip or a special person or an event. Like a visual diary, I can look at any of my cups and remember the day I welcomed it into my home. God reminded me that we're all his precious treasures. He adores us so much that he knows the very day he created us. We are his priceless creations—meant to explore this world, not sit on a protective shelf where we don't experience life.

The woman that morning seemed to have the right

attitude. Instead of leaving her teacup on a shelf to collect dust, she might have been remembering a trip or a special person or an event while enjoying that precious cup. Maybe she uses a different one every day of the week, making every day a special day. What if the teacup she was sipping from that morning was a gift from her mom? The lady in the tattered car could have been as intense about collecting teacups as I am. Perhaps the only difference was that she used hers—what a concept!

I thought about all the other things I collect. I enjoy the thrill in finding a treasure, but now I wonder about the purpose. I doubt whether I'll be buried with all the things I've collected over the years. And I know my son won't cherish them when I'm gone.

I can see the garage sale now! The next owner won't know about the day it rained outside St. Paul's Cathedral in the heart of London as I dodged into the little gift shop to purchase a china teacup. The other bargain shoppers at the garage sale won't know about the time an unknown friend wrapped an antique treasure and gave the teacup to me anonymously. No one will care about the tiny teacup and saucer that was a gift from a ladies retreat I attended years ago. So many teacups and so many stories—stories that matter only to me.

And then God spoke to my heart again. The Bible tells us in Matthew 6:21 that wherever we store our treasures, our hearts will be. I don't want my heart sitting on a cluttered shelf. I want my heart enjoying each and every day God has blessed me with. Nothing is wrong with collectibles, but they're merely fleeting. However, the things I do on earth from my heart will live on.

I've not seen the teacup woman since that day, but every time I enjoy one of my teacup treasures now, I say a silent prayer of thanks for her. I pray that God blesses her like I was blessed that hot summer day.

—Barbara Oden

I GAVE BIRTH TO ALIENS

I understand the popular concept that men and women cannot understand one another because they come from different planets and speak different languages. I understand the concept because I've lived it every single day for the past twenty years. My husband and I don't come from different planets; we come from separate galaxies, maybe even separate universes. I'm a go-with-the-flow, change-the-numbers-to-fit-the-program writer. He's a logical, stick-to-the-numbers engineer. I'm language arts; he's mathematics. I'm spontaneous and fun; he's . . . Did I say I was spontaneous and fun?

Although most of the differences between Rick and me are personality based, not gender related, I came to terms with my husband's unabashed maleness. I even grew to appreciate the differences between the sexes. I just didn't expect those differences to show up in my male offspring.

One of these differences is language. I speak English. They don't. At least, they don't speak it enough. Once they managed that first word, I guess they decided talking wasn't worth the effort.

Studies show that little girls tend to be more verbal than little boys. Memories from my own childhood and observing my daughter at play confirm this. Girls talk the entire time they are playing: "I'll be the next-door neighbor, and I'll knock on the door, and you'll say, 'Come in,' and I'll say, 'OK,' and . . ."

Boys, on the other hand, don't narrate their playing the way girls do. This is not to say that boys are quiet when they play. Oh no! Boys make noise when they play—lots of it. They just don't necessarily use words. They holler, they bellow, they scream in agony when their toy fire truck plunges off an imaginary cliff.

This didn't really become a problem until my boys started school, so I was no longer aware of their every movement throughout the day. "How was your day?" would be met with, "OK." I wanted to know who played with whom at recess, what the teacher wore today, whether the cafeteria fish sticks tasted good, and other pertinent details.

When I asked, "How was your day?" my boys actually thought that was the question they were supposed to answer. They didn't understand that I was really asking, "Did you miss me? Do you still need me?"

Another difference I noticed was that my boys were—and are—fascinated by anything mechanical. I want things to work the way they're supposed to, when they're supposed to. When I start my car, I want the engine to turn over, the air-conditioning to blow cold air, and the radio to play my favorite oldies station. I don't care if my car is fuel injected, if cold air is really the absence of heat (or vice versa), or if radio signals are bounced off Russian satellites and broadcast to the farthest reaches of outer space.

My boys, on the other hand, loved figuring out why and how things work. They loved toys that buzzed and whirred and wailed. They loved taking the toys apart to see why they buzzed and whirred and wailed. The boys loved smashing the pieces with a hammer to see what kind of noise they made while being crushed.

My boys climbed on the furniture, jumped off the furniture, and removed the cushions from the furniture. They used the cushions to construct elaborate mazes all over the living room floor. They piled all the cushions together and jumped onto them from a second-story bedroom loft. They created forts and tents and caves with the cushions.

My boys climbed trees. They caught pollywogs and frogs and kept them in buckets on the back deck. They discovered more uses for scrap wood than Bob Vila on *This Old House*.

They were, in essence, boys—thoroughly, deliciously boys. I know there are girls who climb trees and catch frogs (my daughter, for example). I realize that girls can climb furniture and leap from scary heights. But girls seem to do these things for a reason; it's part of whatever game they're playing at the moment. In contrast, boys seem compelled to do these things for no reason at all. They seem to have an inner voice that says, *Live! Take risks! Turn your mother's hair gray overnight!*

By the time my third son was born, I was accustomed to the noise and chaos active little boys can bring to a house. (Boys, I had learned by then, never walk if they can run, and they never talk if they can shout.)

No, I had grown more than merely accustomed to having little boys. I had begun to like having little boys in the house. I enjoyed the chaos. I found myself admiring their bravado. Sure, they occasionally met with disaster (our local hospital is thinking of dedicating the new emergency room to us as a way of thanking us for all the business we brought in). But, more often, their innocent explorations simply left them tired and dirty.

I decided to embrace what made them different from me, to celebrate the traits that made them gloriously male. I wonder if that's another way we could interpret what the Bible means when it says we should direct our children onto the right path (see Proverbs 22:6).

Traditionally, we interpret this verse to mean that we should direct children in the ways of God so they'll walk in the right spiritual path as they age. And of course that is true—what kind of parents would we be if we neglected our children's spiritual needs? But I wonder if this verse doesn't also encourage parents to direct a child in the way *the child* should *be*—to find what is unique about each individual child and cultivate those special characteristics.

For me, this meant I had to see my sons as future men of God, not just as my little boys. I had to let them be boys because that was how God designed them.

Of course, I'm working to soften the rough edges of their "manly" exteriors so they can function in polite society without dragging their knuckles on the ground. But I want them to keep the spirit of adventure they've always had. I want them to try new things, to risk falling on their faces. I want them to be brave and strong and disciplined, in their minds and in their hearts as well as in their bodies.

And I want them to know that they have a mom who, though she was born in some far away galaxy, has had a very good time visiting their planet.

—Rhonda Wheeler Stock

CONTENTMENT OUTSIDE THE SHOE BOX

What cool shoes! I reached for the tennis shoe on display. The colored trim and the prominent trademark logo sold me immediately. I had to try them on. The clerk brought my size, and I slipped them on. Not only did they look impressive, they cushioned my feet in luxury. I felt so fashionable—even my kids would be impressed!

Being excited by a pair of running shoes was unusual for me. I never understood the pains my teens took when they picked out something as mundane as tennis shoes. My philosophy was to find a decent-looking, inexpensive pair and wear them!

Not *my* boys, though. For them, the shoes' intended purpose, image (especially image), and what shoes their friends wore deeply affected their decision. This decision was so important they were willing to fork over half the cost of the shoes to have something more than I was willing to pay for!

I had set out this morning to purchase my old standard—until these shoes called my name. Now, *I* felt like the teenager. These shoes were definitely nicer looking than the mundane kind I usually bought.

I checked the price. They were twenty dollars more than I usually pay—and twenty dollars over the budget I needed to stick to. I groaned. But I walked around in them a bit more, checked what the slim, trim style looked like from different angles, and felt them soak my feet in comfort.

They're twenty dollars too much. Put them back! I tried to reason my way back to reality. Further, I wondered how I would explain such a purchase to my financial accountability partner, my husband. In our season of life, we needed not only to account for every penny but to wisely spend each one. At other times, the extra twenty dollars wouldn't matter so much, but not now.

Reluctantly, I put the shoes back in the box and left. I checked a couple of other stores for the ones I normally buy. But images of the cool pair lingered in my mind, and I was soon out of the mood to buy anything.

"No shoes?" my husband asked as I arrived home empty handed. Thinking maybe I could find some agreement to splurge just this once, I answered, "You should have seen these shoes I tried on. They looked g-o-o-o-d and felt even better! Coolest shoes in the store."

"How much were they?" When I confessed the price, he laughed. "You'd pay that much for a pair of tennis shoes?"

My frustration immediately returned as I retorted, "Well, as you can see, I didn't buy them, did I?"

I walked off to sulk in self-pity.

Over the next few days, as I put on my old, worn-out tennis shoes, I thought of the shoes I had left behind. Then I thought of our financial situation. I knew God was taking care of us. We had all that we truly needed. But I was growing weary of having to say no to so many things.

A week later my husband and I attended a financial workshop. It was an introduction to a Bible study on finances our church would soon offer. This agitated me even more. We had driven separate cars, so I started home alone. Thoughts of those shoes surfaced again. Thoughts of how I couldn't have them made me begin to cry.

I pounded the steering wheel in anger—anger over tight finances, anger over twenty stinking dollars, anger that I'd let a pair of shoes frustrate me, and anger that I couldn't just forget about them.

The only thing I knew to do was cry to God. "OK, God, I'm tired. I'm tired of fighting against what I can't have. Please, please give me a spirit of contentment. I want to be content with what I can afford and what I already have. I give up the shoes. I put our finances in your hands. Just help me be content."

An unexpected relief consumed me. I wiped the tears. I wondered if I would be able to accept God's contentment and live it day by day. But for now, I knew God had showed me exactly what to pray for—the contentment that had been the missing key to peace in my life.

That evening, armed with a revived spirit, I decided to go purchase my standard replacement tennis shoes. I walked in the store. My eyes fell upon those previously desired shoes. Then, something else caught my attention. A big, red sticker with a sale price—$20 off! The clerk seemed a bit wary of this grown woman so excited about a tennis-shoe purchase!

Do I think God will turn the tables every time I pour out my heart to him in anger? Do I feel God rewarded my submission to his ways? Although God's Word reminds us that he will bless our obedience, I think I might run the risk of becoming a spiritual brat if everything always turned out my way. Rather, I believe God is motivated by his glory. He chose to "rescue" his chosen people, the Israelites, time and again, simply so his glory and authority would be revealed. His rescues were signs that he is in total control of this universe. In one of those instances God declared, "I am bringing you back, but not because you deserve it. I am doing it to protect my holy name" (Ezekiel 36:22).

I saw God's hand in my shoe episode. I just happened to receive an extra blessing out of it too: Each time I put on my shoes, I remember the grace, goodness, and glory of my powerful Father.

Being reminded that God is in control helps me live a life of contentment. Experiencing the Creator of the universe working in my life reminds me of what is really important—a relationship with him in which I can be honest in everything.

—Karen Morerod

FALLING INTO THE ARMS OF LOVE

You live through some moments in slow motion. That's what happened as I was tumbling down the stairs headfirst.

I'd been holding on to the rail. But then my heel caught in the carpet, and my computer bag—slung over my left shoulder—swung forward when I tripped. Without that, I might have recovered my balance, but the heavy, swinging load cooperated with gravity to pull me forward and propel me down.

To keep from hitting my noggin on the wall at the end of the landing, I ducked. I broke my collarbone, banged up my shoulder, and maybe fractured a couple of ribs, too, though at the time no one could tell for sure.

Our daughter, Alexandra, was playing in the backyard. Usually at 5:10 P.M., the time it happened, she and I had the place to ourselves. However, my mother-in-law, who had come to help Alexandra with homework, heard me scream and ran to my rescue.

I couldn't get up on my own.

My husband, Gary, usually arrives home around six but had left the office a little early to get home and cover child care while I went to deliver a ninety-minute lecture on bioethics. So when I called Gary, he was only about ten minutes from home.

While I writhed and waited, I tried to contact the professor whose class I was supposed to teach. After several attempts, I reached him.

When Gary arrived home, I took one look at his concerned face and fell in love all over again.

"Where do you want me to take you?" he asked, treating a hospital choice as if he were plotting a dinner date.

"Baylor. Downtown."

"It takes longer to get there. Why not the local one?"

The place that had misdiagnosed our daughter's broken elbow sometime earlier? Not a chance.

So he drove me to Dallas's Baylor emergency room while Grammy cared for Alexandra.

I could feel and see the break; the bone sticking up under the skin told me I had more than a sprain. But what evoked real fear was the pain I felt when I exhaled. I hoped I didn't have a rib poking into a lung.

The thirty-minute drive—filled with tears, moans, and *kyrie eleisons* (prayers for mercy)—felt like it took a month. Then we walked into the ER and found a crowd of about thirty people ahead of us. I imagined myself sitting there for three hours.

Please, no!

The triage nurse asked what had happened. I told her I'd fallen down the steps. To my amazement, she looked me in the eye and said, "I'm so sorry," before asking my name and insurance coverage. I was a person, not a case, not a shoulder injury, not a potential punctured lung.

Nothing makes me want to bawl like a little empathy. *Keep it together, keep it together,* I mentally repeated. The nurses took one look at me, all wobbly, breathing fast, moaning, with my right shoulder an inch higher than my left—which they even noted aloud—and ushered me right into a room. Then I didn't know if I should rejoice that I got to the head of the line or despair that they considered my injury serious.

Over the next six hours, technicians shot X-rays of my collarbone. It was broken. Royally. Then they took X-rays of my chest and drew blood to make sure I was up for a CAT scan. I was. I drank the syrupy, grape-flavored metal stuff designed to light up my innards for the machine.

Once the medical team gave me the all clear that there was no internal bleeding, they pumped me full of painkillers (finally!), giving me something that made me loopy.

They saw no cracked ribs, though they said I might have a few. They recommended rest—lots of rest—and meds for the pain.

That's the medical side. The rest of it was better. Seriously better.

The men's group, which was meeting at our church when my husband called from the ER to tell somebody what was happening, headed down to the hospital to hang out with us.

When we called home from the ER, Grammy said, "Alexandra is in bed, and I'm lying next to her on the floor."

I didn't have time to stop and ponder such grand-parently love before she added, "Alexandra says to tell Mommy she loves her and that the kitties send their love too."

Wow, the cats love me. Who knew?

The prayer chain sent out e-mail messages. People prayed.

The following afternoon, a meal arrived, apparently the first of a bunch that people would deliver for the next six weeks—a full thirty days after we told people they could stop feeding us.

People sent me e-mails. Some added silly photo attachments to cheer me. Others phoned. My niece even baked a cake for me.

The chaplain of Dallas Seminary, where I work, called, and his prayer made me laugh and cry—laugh, because he joked; cry, because through his words I felt God's presence and tender love.

The church is Christ's body—his arms hugging and nourishing and loving. Our brothers and sisters loved us well, showing up as Jesus-with-skin-on. We are not alone.

Yes, I took a nasty fall—right into the arms of love.

—Sandra Glahn

AFRICAN CHOW MEIN, ANYONE?

Cooking can feed a soul as well as fill a stomach. But perhaps God specially blesses a cook when she uses a recipe from a church cookbook.

When I offered to help plan for the youth-group mission trip to Trinidad, I agreed to do anything but fund-raising. God had other ideas. Two weeks later, I represented one-third of a three-woman fund-raising committee charged with producing a church cookbook for our two-thousand-member church in less than three months. Coordinating an all-church spaghetti supper joined our "To Do" list a week later.

When a pastor calls for recipes from the pulpit, the results just may be surprising. Sharing favorite family recipes provides an insider's look into fellow church members' kitchens. The more than eight hundred submissions reflected societal and generational trends as well as seventeen variations of broccoli salad and twelve versions of beef brisket.

I didn't expect God to use the cookbook project to remind me that people aren't always what they seem. For example, take the older woman who stopped faithfully at the recipe-collection table set up Sundays in the fellowship hall, promising she wouldn't forget to bring her favorite recipe the next week. Without a doubt, I had her pegged in the Jell-O salad generation.

Many great cooks and bakers are found in this group, but some members specialize in downright frightening concoctions, such as Eight-Can Casserole. This flexible recipe contains multiple cans of anything that can be found in the dusty, distant back of the pantry, layered in a 13 x 9-inch Pyrex casserole dish. Another unforgettable recipe attributed to this sector is the Fiesta Spam Loaf, which layers Spam and mashed canned yams, topped with slices of canned peaches arranged in a pinwheel formation. So far, we hadn't received either of these infamous recipes for the cookbook.

However, this woman's generation typically is the source for myriad molded Jell-O salad recipes. These call for ingredients ranging from sauerkraut, applesauce, and green olives to chipped beef, crushed pineapple, and cottage cheese, suspended together in harvest-gold gelatin. Baby boomers like myself, who grew up with kitchen walls adorned with gleaming copper Jell-O molds, tend to avoid this salad genre, although I do respect the time and energy it takes to create these layered beauties, even more, to successfully get them out of the mold. The Jell-O molds I received for wedding presents, however, have received only an occasional use when I freeze decorative ice rings for the punch bowl at a baby shower or an Eagle Scout court of honor.

Regardless, I was expecting Jell-O. But on deadline Sunday, this woman triumphantly turned in her cherished recipe—for Tofu Enchiladas.

The same day, she brought her dog-eared copy of our church's last cookbook, published in 1964. The organization of the book intrigued me. The first and largest section? Desserts. And the small mimeographed booklet did, indeed, contain a voluminous section of congealed salads. Reflecting the custom of the day, all married recipe contributors were listed using their husbands' names, as if Mr. Walter Nobringer would really want to be associated with his wife's cholesterol-busting deviled egg and crushed potato-chip casserole. I was glad the real cooks in our new cookbook would receive the proper recognition they were due.

Sorting recipes reminded me how closely food and family are connected. Many recipes were titled by the name of someone special: Grandma Helen's Butter Cookies, Grammy Mary's Cherry Cheesecake, Meredith's Yum-Yums, Honor-Your-Mother Brownies.

Just as the smell of ginger and cinnamon takes me back to my grandmother's kitchen and her homemade cookies, family recipes keep memories alive and preserve tastes as well as traditions, generation after generation. Sharing fellowship over meals has been a hallmark of the Christian church from the time of the apostles to today's small groups, and who knows when the first church-potluck recipe was swapped? Our church members took recipe selection seriously.

However, the more I was thinking about food and cooking, the more my family was eating take-out meals. Several weeks later, after being flooded with recipes for sweets, breads, and salads, we began requesting recipes to fill out the other sections. Somehow, side dishes don't hold the same sentimental significance, but we wanted a more-balanced book than our forty-year-old predecessor. As we collected preorders along with the recipes, the prospects of raising significant funds to offset the ambitious high-school mission trip looked good.

Winning our Presbyterian popularity contest were potato casseroles, baked beans, chocolate-chip cookies, sugar cookies, quick breads, and pastas—tangible evidence that the low-carbohydrate trend continues to decline. The Midwest is still comfort-food country, although the contributions were far more cosmopolitan than in 1964. Only a few lonely Jell-O salad recipes appeared in our submission box, primarily cranberry versions representing family Christmas traditions as long standing as the Christmas Eve candlelight service. Many recipes showcased ethnic specialties or international cuisine trends. But a quick reading of the ingredients showed one dish was submitted simply using a globe-trotting disguise. Take a bite of African Chow Mein and you're sampling yet another hamburger-rice casserole, with soy sauce the only ingredient even hinting at the exotic.

Our deadline looming, the three of us met, fittingly, at our dining room tables, surrounded by stacks of recipes. As savvy shoppers, we knew pre-Christmas sales represented our best market. A church cookbook containing several of one's own specialties is almost as good a gift as a plate of homemade Christmas cookies. We had promised delivery before Christmas, and we were praying we'd make it.

Naively, we had allotted only a few meetings to sort the recipes into sections, not realizing what a challenge it would be. The cookbook production company we were using allowed only a certain number of sections for us to get the cheapest production price. We deliberated putting soups before salads, or cookies before cakes. Where do those pesky brunch dishes fit in when you're out of separate headings? Is homemade granola a bread? How do you alphabetize Marty's Kansas Christmas Sugar Cookies? Finally, we added a Miscellaneous section, photocopied and packaged the whole thing, and mailed it off in faith.

Several weeks later, the widow of our church's beloved former senior pastor called. She had just returned from an extended trip and had several recipes to submit if possible. When she heard that the book had already gone to print, she insisted that we not make any extra effort, but I called the cookbook company anyway to check on adding a few more recipes. No one at the company had ever heard of the project. I alternated between praying and panicking. A pre-Christmas delivery suddenly seemed impossible.

The next day, a company representative called to apologize. The box of recipes had been found, tucked in a forgotten corner of the mail room. Typesetting would begin immediately, we would be sent proofs within two weeks, and yes, we should receive our shipment of one thousand books before Thanksgiving. The company representative was so grateful I had called. At church on Sunday, I told the pastor's wife God had used her in a mighty way.

We blessed the cookbook company when the books arrived, right on time. My committee cohorts, both of them accountants, set up computerized spreadsheets that made tracking distribution and checks easier, particularly important because our church has two campuses. Preorders were snapped up, and sales were brisk. The recipe for Black Russian Cake created a small stampede of members buying the cookbook after that chocolate beauty was brought to a Sunday school class Christmas party. Cookbook sales on Sunday morning also became endorsement sessions, as members stopped by to share new favorites they had tried from the book that week.

Chatting during a slow sales morning with the member minding the next table over, I mentioned that I personally was uninspired by the recipe that called for blowing up balloons, coating them in chocolate, and decorating and then chilling the inflated balloons, as if I would have room for them in my refrigerator. The elaborate instructions then called for deflating and successfully removing the balloons from unbroken shells, followed by filling the chocolate globes with perfectly dipped fruit or homemade mousse. She, however, was entranced by the idea and bought a cookbook just to try it out.

As Christmas neared, our supplies dwindled. Youth hoping to go on the mission trip carried trays of homemade Christmas cookies (recipes in the book, of course) and cookbooks through the foyer. With no more Sundays before Christmas, only a few boxes remained. By mid-January, they were gone.

Months later, hearing the experiences of the twenty-five youth and adults who spent a week working and sharing the gospel in the housing projects, orphanages, and prisons of the poor island of Trinidad, I was grateful God had given me the opportunity to play a part. The trip was truly life changing for students, opening their eyes to God's power and the needs of his children around the world. Hard physical labor and stepping far beyond their comfort zones had taught the students much in a short time. God worked in amazing ways.

A cookbook has a long shelf life. I smile when members stop me in the balcony to mention they love my recipe for my mother's Congo Bars or tell me that they just tried something new from the book this week. We still get calls wondering if there are any left. Perhaps some years ahead, it will be time for a sequel to support a new crop of student missionaries. Maybe the time will be right for a behind-the-scenes book:

discovering the secrets of Tracy's Miss Texas Casserole or the roots of Watergate Salad. Whoever invented that hash-brown casserole, anyway? And of course, the second volume would solve the mystery of African Chow Mein, tracing its origins around the world and finally finding its birthplace somewhere like North Dakota. Just don't serve it with Jell-O.

—Sue Lowell Gallion

"Oh no, here we go again." I raced to the bathroom.

Yes, I can make it, I told myself. *Just one more corner.*

I threw open the door just in time and slid around the corner, tossing my cookies and my left shoe.

Oh, the joys of pregnancy.

"You'll love it," I had been told—"Nothing better than being pregnant."

Pooh. Bless those women who don't get sick during pregnancy. But for those of us who do, the first trimester's not easy. Whoever coined the term "morning sickness" had to be a man. You feel sick all day long, not just in the mornings.

OK, yes, I know I asked for this, even prayed for this. But weeks of nausea, exhaustion, backaches, and headaches can make anyone irritable. On the brighter side, I lost five pounds—though pregnancy is not a diet plan I recommend or would even wish on my worst enemy.

I was having one of those cranky days, when God sent me an angel.

After another wave of nausea, I thought about what I'd gotten myself into. I was thirty-six years old, a married, working woman with a precious four-year-old. My husband and I were past the diapers and disposable pants phase. She was sleeping by herself, and I finally had some "me time." What on earth was I thinking when we agreed to have another child?

Now I was going down the road to motherhood all over again. My back, abdomen, and other parts ached; I couldn't eat very much; and all I wanted to do was sleep. I washed out my mouth, only to get the sensation again and doubled over. I knelt there, with my face flushed and my eyes watering, thinking *Poor me,* when I heard a voice and felt a soft hand on my back.

"Jesus, please help my mommy feel better," this sweet voice said.

A tear welled up in my eye and cascaded down my face. My four-year-old daughter gazed at me with concern and love on her little face.

"You OK, Mommy?" she asked.

"Yes, sweetie. It's just that the baby is making Mommy sick right now."

She looked at me again, then kissed me on the cheek. "I love you—hope you feel better soon."

"Mommy does too." Brushing another tear from my cheek, I hugged her. "I love you, too. Do you know how special you are?"

She smiled, her dimpled face glowing. "Yeah."

I dragged myself up from the bathroom floor. I hugged her again, washed my face, and used some mouthwash. My daughter needed dinner, and I needed a few crackers and a soda for my stomach.

As I entered the kitchen, the joys of motherhood surrounded me. On the refrigerator, my daughter's Sunday school projects were proudly displayed. Beside them were pictures depicting wonderful times our family had spent together. And scattered in between were little notes that said, "I love you, Mommy."

I smiled as I gathered sandwich supplies. Glancing at the pictures on the fridge door one last time, I picked up the sandwich, placed it and some chips on a plate, then headed toward the living room. Exhausted from this one little task, I gave the sandwich to my daughter and slumped in a chair.

"You feeling better, Mommy?"

"Kind of." I bit a cracker and closed my eyes as Looney Tunes echoed through my aching head. Feeling a warm hand on mine, I opened them.

"Jesus, help Mommy." Taking a bite of her sandwich, she hugged me. Her soft cheek rested on my chest. "Mommy, you smell nice."

A tear came to my eye as I hugged her back. "Thank you, sweetheart. Mommy loves you so much."

"I love you, too." She held on tight for a few minutes before the call of the cartoon drew her back from my embrace.

She was once again immersed in the world of a four-year-old, but her words couldn't have meant more. I was tired and felt disgusting and sick, but to my daughter, I smelled good. It was as if the Lord had sent my daughter to remind me of the wonderful gift soon to be birthed from my struggle—a special gift, a loving child. Seeing my daughter's beautiful eyes, her smile, and her funny laugh reminded me of the blessings that come with motherhood.

I can't see him or her; yet the small child growing inside needs me. My present situation should not change or cloud the love that went into conceiving this child—a love that I must focus on, even though the reward is still months away.

I continued to gaze at my little inspiration, thinking, *I'd do anything for her, even die for her. Wow!* I thought, *The plight of motherhood is like the wait we endure for the rewards of heaven.* Some rewards we can see right now, but many we won't see till we get there. God reminded me to see past the months of nausea, pain, and discomfort I was enduring before my child's birth to my future treasures in heaven. He reminded me that he is preparing a wonderful place for me. He knows my pain, and he knows the reward is near. The time of my struggle is short compared to the many years of joy I will receive from my nine months of pregnancy.

I glanced at my daughter and saw a smile cross her shimmering face. I smiled, too, closing my tired eyes as my hand rested on my belly.

Lord, thank you. Thank you for sending me lessons through the mouth of a child. Thank you for sending me words of inspiration uttered from the sweet lips of my four-year-old. And with those tender thoughts permeating my tired soul and body, I drifted off to sleep—secure that God was in control, that today's struggles would reap future blessings.

—Arnita C. Wright

LOVE CONQUERS ALL THINGS

Bam! My husband, John, hurled my new sewing machine to the floor. We'd been married only a month when I accused him of flirting with his secretary. John and I had argued many times, but this time I provoked him beyond his limit.

I stormed out of our apartment, sobbing. *Where should I go?* I wondered. Generations of divorce had filled both sides of my family and created my deep-seated mistrust of men. Now, I was already entertaining thoughts of divorce.

As I climbed into my '69 Volkswagen bug, Tom and Sue flashed through my mind. Tom was our new auto insurance agent. Perceiving significant needs in our marriage, he and his wife had befriended us. They frequently invited us to dinner and sporting events, and for the first time in my life, I had observed a marriage in which both partners modeled respect for each other.

I shivered at our friends' doorstep while I gathered enough courage to knock. Tom invited me in, and between sobs I spilled exaggerated stories about John's faults. Instead of supporting me to leave John, Sue held my hand and reassured me that everything was going to work out. She encouraged me to forgive John. I swallowed my pride and returned home, but I held on to my resentment.

A week later, we accepted Tom's invitation to go to church. Warm welcomes invaded my personal comfort zone. When we received a visitor's card, John printed our names, but I made sure he *didn't* check the box that requested a pastor's visit.

However, the next day the telephone rang. "Hi. This is Pastor Andy from Stratford Community Bible Church. Could I visit you tonight?" he asked, and John agreed.

That evening Pastor Andy shared stories about his hippie days in the sixties. He even admitted that he had threatened his wife with a knife.

What kind of a preacher is this guy? I wondered. But when he explained how God had transformed his life and saved his marriage, my suspicions dissolved. Pastor Andy turned to John and asked, "Do you think you're going to heaven?"

"Well, I think so," John stammered. "I'm a pretty good guy. I don't drink much, and I don't swear much. I do more good than bad."

I echoed John's response, adding, "If John's going to heaven, surely I'm going because I drink and swear a lot less than he does!"

"That's not good enough," Andy said.

I fidgeted while Andy opened his Bible and asked us to listen: "Everyone has sinned; we all fall short of God's glorious standard. . . . The wages of sin is death, but the free gift of God is eternal life through Christ Jesus our Lord" (Romans 3:23; 6:23).

"Do you understand that Jesus' death on the cross paid the penalty for your sins?" he asked. He then turned to Romans 10:9 and read, "If you confess with your mouth that Jesus is Lord and believe in your heart that God raised him from the dead, you will be saved."

Andy put a question to us: "Do you want to be saved from your sins and know for sure you're going to heaven?" It seemed almost too easy. Why hadn't I ever heard this before?

John's eyes met mine, and together we expressed our desire for eternal life. We quietly repeated Pastor Andy's prayer and then rose from our knees fully forgiven.

That evening ushered in hope for healing our marriage. We began attending church regularly and joined a young couples' Bible study. We gained insights and tools to help our marriage. Yet I still struggled. Now that John had come to Christ, I figured he'd meet all my expectations. When he didn't, I responded critically. I thought I was justified in my displeasure. "But," someone once told me, "marriage isn't about finding the right person, it's about becoming the right person."

For the next eight years, I poured my energy into raising a family. Homeschooling four children occupied me so that I had less time to dwell on hurts and disappointments. Occasionally, however, I entertained pity parties. "My needs aren't being met!" I whined.

That's when I began journaling. It became my emotional outlet when I got upset. Every secret complaint against John was recorded in my journal.

As my faith matured, I couldn't get away with blaming. I realized my need to change. God was calling me to give up my rights, my excuses, my reasons, my explanations, and my defenses. This new understanding of how to love my husband was soon tested when it came time to make vacation plans.

Because we were expecting our fifth child, a perfect family vacation for me meant relaxing in a nearby cabin, nestled in the woods and far from relatives and friends. However, John wanted to travel. He wanted to visit his sisters and mother, who live hundreds of miles away. When he talked about scouting out childhood stomping grounds and attending his family's annual reunion, I put my foot down.

"I want to rest and relax," I countered. "Can't we go someplace peaceful and quiet, away from relatives?"

After repeated debates, I finally gave in. God showed me that loving John meant putting his interests ahead of my own. Halfheartedly, I packed our suitcases.

When we reached our destination, Green Bay, Wisconsin, we skipped from home to home, visiting relatives I hardly knew. My impatience mounted, and so did my feelings of neglect. Consequently, I began mentally recording a list of complaints. Exercising my old habit of keeping an account of John's shortcomings quickly nurtured new seeds of resentment that sprouted into bitterness. One evening after tucking the kids in bed, I caved in and fired off my list of frustrations.

Instead of acting defensively or starting an argument, John simply asked what he could do to help. Then he purchased an airplane ticket for me to fly home. By putting my needs first and sparing me ten hours in a van full of rambunctious kids, John showed me a perfect example of God's unconditional love.

When I arrived home, I retreated to my bedroom. I sat in silence, inhaling and exhaling slowly. Gradually, the tension left my muscles, and my head fell limp.

"Please help me," I prayed.

In spite of my grumpiness, God met me. He lavished his love upon me, reminding me that nothing could separate me from his love, not even my short temper and critical spirit. Tears trickled down my cheeks.

Nestled in God's safe, loving arms, my heart softened. With the Holy Spirit's help, I focused on my sins instead of my husband's shortcomings. God's laser exposed each negative thought and word. One by one, I confessed them and asked for forgiveness. That day I stopped recording John's wrongs in my journal.

God's power renewed my strength. I asked him to continue to operate in my life so I could love sacrificially, forgive those who sinned against me, speak the truth in love, and overcome evil with good. The black cloud shadowing me diminished.

Over the past thirty years of marriage, I've continued to journal; however, I no longer keep score of hurts and disappointments. Now, I choose to pay close attention to John's kind words and thoughtful actions. I record them on a page in my journal I've labeled my "brag list." It includes small stuff, such as when John opens the car door for me or reaches for my hand when we go for a walk. I keep track of the special moments—when I'm watching TV and he gets up to serve my favorite soda, or when he calls me at work just to say, "I'm thinking of you."

Love flourishes whenever I let meekness and humility take over.

This past summer we drove to beautiful Mackinac Island. Traveling there left me exhausted, so John offered to take our 13-year-old daughter to Starbucks while I soaked in a hot bubble bath.

My fondest memory is when my husband got up early one morning to jog while I stayed in bed reading a book.

When he returned, he gave me a wild, long-stemmed iris, its pale lavender petals sprinkled with dew. Holding the flower in one hand and a cup of my favorite hot tea in the other, he said, "Here, honey. When I saw this flower, it reminded me of you."

Since I've put resentment aside, I've learned the truth of 1 Corinthians 13. Now, that's my checklist for my relationship with my husband, and I've learned firsthand that when it comes to tough times in marriage, love can conquer all.

—Pamela Enderby

While we were enjoying a peaceful meal as a family, my husband leaned forward to ask a question.

"Honey, have you just recently brushed your hair?"

"No, why?" I asked, curious.

"I don't know. It looks different, like you just brushed it or something."

I smiled when I realized the comment was his way of saying he knew something had changed. Hmmm. Maybe my complete hairstyle—four days ago.

Then, that night while I put my youngest daughter to bed, she, too, complimented my hair (at least I think it was a compliment) and said in her sweetest voice, "Mommy, I like your hair. It looks so windy."

"Well, thank you, honey, but I think you mean to say it looks wispy?"

With an adamant shake of the head, she stated, "No, I don't."

So, last night while I was lying in bed counting curlers, I began to wonder if I should take my family's observations as compliments or criticisms. I mean, quite honestly, I can't recall the last time I meandered up to a girlfriend and said, "I love your hair; it looks so . . . um . . . recently brushed and windy!"

I think we women crave a good word now and then. Our hearts long to hear affirmation and gushy compliments, even if the gushing is a little over the top—sweet and exaggerated. A good word tastes s-o-o-o good to the soul.

Besides being satisfying, words can be versatile. Let's think about this: We can eat our words, regret them, deny them, weigh them. We can even play with them, *but* try to tame them! Two months ago I started studying a book that focused on taming the tongue. I have to admit, I broke a sweat in the first two chapters and have scarcely been able to continue. Yes, for me taming my speech is a little like taming wild horses. And words and wild horses do not always go together.

I learned that firsthand a few weeks ago.

My family and I decided to enjoy a refreshing day at a Kentucky horse farm. Wide open blankets of bluegrass with white lace fences—this was always a great day of togetherness for us. And the highlight? Horseback riding.

Now, being a novice with horses and having had a few anxious experiences with the large creatures, I marked myself in red as a beginner on the rider application, with hopes of saddling a calm equine.

If there was any doubt about my lack of horsewoman know-how, it was quickly erased as I attempted to mount Ranger backward. Oops—wrong foot in the stirrup!

Yes, even the kind horse handler agreed that saddling backward would have made for an interesting ride for both the horse and me.

Detecting my apprehension to go any further with the fiasco, the cowboy convinced me that a few nice words and a looser grip on the reins would result in a pleasant, uneventful ride. A cowboy should know, right? Uh-huh.

Yes, initially all was well. I relaxed on the reins, while my words were sweeter than sugar cubes—until another horse bit mine in the behind. Ranger bucked high into the air, propelling my body forward and my nose to my knees. Yikes!

Now, at age forty, I can assure you that my nose doesn't voluntarily touch my knees. Oh no. For me to achieve this movement usually requires a certain amount of coaxing and a whole lot of momentum. A little more force and my foot would have literally been in my mouth.

As quick as a swift wind, my words turned cold, and I was yelling to my son (who happened to be four horses behind me) to hold onto his saddle for dear life! I don't know why, but no one else appeared to be at the heightened state of alarm that I was. In fact, the rest of the line kept moseying along the trail without missing a hoofbeat. And I'm not sure, but I think the woman in front of me flashed a scowl when my horse got out of order and passed hers. I mean, can I help it if she landed the horse I wanted, the one that appeared to suffer from some type of horse narcolepsy? Lucky lady.

So not only are words a necessity to feed the soul, but they have the power to build up and the power to warn. And I find affirming words so essential that I literally have had times in my life when I felt starved for a word of encouragement.

One such time was a few years ago when our daughter was seriously ill. She had had brain surgery and could not handle a great deal of noise without getting a nauseating headache. So, the Duewel Zoo—as we so fondly refer to our home—became a house of calm and quiet. No hustle to and from activities, no giggling till our ears ached, no stories, and no sibling squabbles (I can't believe I actually missed that).

What remained was a home filled with walls of quiet. It was enough to make this word-hungry woman want to scream.

To add to the stress, everyone in the family got the stomach flu except our seriously ill daughter. Little could be said to lessen our family's pain. Friends and family rallied with love and hope, but it all seemed to disappear like water through sand and left my soul an empty pit.

Unable to ignore the "hunger pains" any longer, I remembered how in the past God's words had reached my depths. Famished, I turned page after page of the Bible, feeling God's Spirit fill my void and give me hope. My appetite for his Word became insatiable. Psalm 119:103 tells of God's ability to feed the soul: "How sweet your words taste to me; they are sweeter than honey."

Now when I speak a word, I remember the nourishment and hope it can dish out: the sweetness of Christ's communion through the power of his Word.

Well . . . a hair appointment awaits me. In fact, I think I'm ready for a change. Maybe a "breezy" look this time!

—Beth Duewel

NOT YET

Age is one of those things we women don't like to disclose, although I'm not quite sure why. Shouldn't we be happy that we've lived this long? I admit that at times I've fudged about my age. But after a few decades of birthdays—and those painful life lessons that accompany them—I'm no longer evasive or embarrassed about acknowledging my age of fifty-three. I look at it as a rite of passage. Hey, I've earned these wrinkles and gray hairs.

Even so, for me, getting older has not been without its issues.

Turning fifty wasn't traumatic. It was my forty-ninth birthday that caused distress. It started when I went for a routine checkup and my doctor found that not only did I have hypothyroidism (now a real excuse for my sluggish metabolism and inability to lose weight!), but my blood indicated higher-than-normal liver enzyme levels.

OK, no big deal. Medication takes care of that—right? For the thyroid problem, yes, which means taking medication for the rest of my life. But the liver issue was more serious. It could mean liver disease or the very worst—cancer. My doctor scheduled an ultrasound. What did she find? Nothing—absolutely nothing.

She sent me to a gastroenterologist. He couldn't find a

reasonable explanation, either, so he scheduled a liver biopsy. If you've never had one, don't believe anyone who tells you it's nothing. The doctor inserts a needle into your liver, which is on the right just below your rib cage, and retrieves liver tissue. You have to remain still so the doctor doesn't accidentally nick your lung or gallbladder. Every time the doctor inserts the needle, you have to hold your breath until you feel like your chest cavity will explode.

After I had endured this procedure, what was the specialist's report? Inconclusive. He could say only that carrying around my extra weight probably contributed to the liver anomalies.

Did I do anything about my weight?

"Not yet," I told God. "But I will, as soon as the weather is nice and I can get outside."

Around this time I began having night sweats and hot flashes. Then I lost my job, due to downsizing. I wasn't even fifty, but I was falling apart.

Did I change?

"Not yet," I told God. "I need more time to figure out who I am."

When I turned fifty-two, I had another checkup and blood test. The results: high cholesterol. My cholesterol had always been low, so this surprised me. Now I had one more medication to remember to take.

I lamented to God about my physical woes, but did I change?

"Not yet," I told God. "I want to see if these meds help."

I had been letting my health slip for years, particularly after the death of my mom seven years earlier. I exercised occasionally and promised myself I'd do better the next day or week or month, but of course, that didn't happen.

Then last year, my father's congestive heart-failure condition worsened, and I spent most of my time at his bedside—time that I spent eating fast food, not exercising, not sleeping, not going to church faithfully, and not spending quality time with God. My prayers were mostly limited to "Please take care of Dad."

After Dad died, I was appointed executor of his estate. This meant more responsibility and even less time to take care of me. Instead, I spent my time handling his affairs, and when I wasn't doing that, I sat in my recliner and wept.

I knew I'd feel better if I'd do something about my health, but did I?

"Not yet, God. I need time to grieve."

My grip on life was slipping. Sorrow, anger, sadness, complacency—all sorts of emotions hit me. I knew part of it was because I was grieving for my dad, but there was something else.

A couple of months after Dad died, I had another doctor's appointment and more blood work to recheck my liver function.

After the dreaded weigh-in, my doctor's first comments were about another patient who had similar health problems: a sedentary lifestyle and overweight with high cholesterol.

"Last week my patient dropped dead of a heart attack," she told me.

That got my attention. But what did God hear from me?

"Not yet, God. I'm not ready to die."

I thought about this for days afterward and realized I couldn't avoid my problems anymore. My dad had high blood pressure, high cholesterol, and heart disease. My oldest brother had similar problems. I could see the genetic writing on the wall. How long had I pretended the writing was too blurry to read? It was clearly in focus now and written in God's hand.

Until then, his words had penetrated my mind but not my heart. I had failed to see that God could be a *big* part of my solution. Before, I had tried to rely on my own strength to change. Now God said, "OK, your way hasn't worked. Now how about trying my way?"

What did God hear from me this time?

"OK, God, I'm ready. Show me the way."

God didn't send a solution, but he did send a revelation: I had put off taking care of myself, hoping my circumstances would change. News flash from heaven: That will *never* happen. If I was going to get in shape, eat better, and nurture my spiritual well-being, I had to do these things no matter what else happened.

I had promised myself so many times to exercise, eat better, and care about and for myself. This time, I would follow through. This time, I would surrender to God and allow him to show me how.

Luckily (or maybe it wasn't coincidence?), I work for a university where I could use its health-care facilities and services. I hired a personal trainer, starting with ten sessions to see if my body would respond or go into shock from years of inactivity. Every Tuesday and Thursday I met with my trainer, Ashley, a diminutive strawberry blonde with a dynamic personality and boundless energy. Exactly what I needed.

She encouraged me, pushed me, challenged me, empathized with me, and respected me and my newfound mission. But most of all, she kept me focused on taking care of myself, which also included not beating myself up if I slipped now and then. She placed the emphasis on getting fit and healthy rather than on weight. If I lost weight, that was a bonus.

After ten more sessions, Ashley deemed me ready to go it alone. Since then, I have not only lost inches and a few pounds but gained back my long-absent self-esteem. Clothes fit better, and I have more energy. My husband and I are also eating healthier: more poultry, fish, and vegetables and less red meat and processed foods.

I know I'll never weigh what I weighed in high school or after my second son was born (size 8, I hardly remember you), and I still have more "junk in my trunk" than I'd like, but I'm working on it. I may never run a marathon, but I am finally comfortable in my own skin.

Perhaps when I started this program, I was hoping to drop a ton of weight, but now after being on a regular exercise regime, my health and well-being is much more important.

Looking back to where my journey began, I had another revelation: Age and poor health don't have to be companions. My age was not to blame for my health problems; neglecting my physical well-being for decades was. I thank God that he opened both my physical and my spiritual eyes to see what my future would hold if I didn't change my unhealthful ways.

This wasn't about vanity; it was about taking care of the body God has loaned me so I can better serve him. It's also about honoring the temple in which the Holy Spirit lives.

Now when the time comes for God to welcome me into his Kingdom, he won't hear me say, "Not yet, God."

Instead, he will hear, "OK, God, I'm ready. Show me the way."

—C J Hines

THE GREETING CARD

Hmph, hmph.

Vanessa's grunts were right on schedule. I tried to ignore her audible tokens of disapproval and continued worshiping in the service.

Vanessa's grunts had begun not too long after my husband and I first joined the church a few years earlier. At first I thought it was my imagination. But the next Sunday, more of the same sounds flowed from Vanessa and seemed to beeline straight to me. This time the sounds were accompanied by a rolling of the eyes and hateful looks. I smiled and said good morning to everyone around me. Through all the good morning replies, I couldn't help but notice that Vanessa's was not one of them.

My husband says I'm a sensitive soul. I guess when you have been through painful happenings in life, either you learn to let stuff not bother you or you become oversensitive as a protective measure to ward off pain. And like most people, I was no stranger to pain, emotional or physical.

To be honest, sometimes I have offended people unintentionally. My grandmother always said, "You have to be careful that your mouth don't give your rear end a bad name."

I think I understand that saying clearly now. I speak

sometimes fully meaning one thing when I start and communicating something totally different in the end. So, aware that I sometimes misinterpret what was meant, I decided to ignore Vanessa's little grunts.

This continued for weeks. I tried different things to start a conversation with her. If she answered at all, it was always with one word, making sure no conversation followed.

One Sunday, I decided to leave home early so I could choose a different seat. Another time, I intentionally made us late trying to get a seat away from Vanessa. I tried everything to sit anywhere she was not. However late or early we were, somehow Vanessa's seat was near my seat. One thing I have learned is that when God wants to teach you something, you can't get away from it.

I tried to figure out why she didn't like me. Being a light-skinned black female, sometimes I felt as if I experienced discrimination from all sides. I felt that I was not dark enough for some or not light enough for others and that no one wanted to see beyond the outer package. Perhaps that was what bothered Vanessa.

But no, I checked this off my list pretty soon as I observed her talking to other ladies of all sizes, shapes, ages, and complexions.

Maybe I did do something to make her not like me. Maybe I slipped with my tongue and said something offensive without realizing it. I searched through my mind, scanning encounter after encounter I'd had with her during the previous months. I came up with nothing.

Vanessa's grunts and obvious disapproval still bothered me. It's funny how if someone in the community or at work would say something that hurt my feelings I could easily let it go. I guess I expected the people of the world to be hurtful, but when a sister in Christ acts this way, the pain penetrates my not-so-thick skin. As I pondered the problem of Vanessa, I thought, *We are supposed to be Christians, loving each other.*

Then, as I prayed during one service, asking God to forgive me if I had done anything to offend this lady, I suddenly felt it wasn't my problem. I was sure I had done nothing to make her treat me in such a way, and if I had, it was not intentional.

I thought of Dr. Martin Luther King Jr. and his peace walk, and I realized I was suffering nothing but hurt feelings. People would spit in Dr. King's face, and he was able to walk in peace. Clearly Dr. King's close relationship to Jesus strengthened him to withstand the injustice he faced. His legacy shows us how to be quick to forgive and patient with others for Christ's sake. Dr. King followed Jesus' example, showing us that other people's attitudes and actions may hurt, but we can walk in peace.

God was still playing his musical-chair game—week after week Vanessa and I ended up sitting near each other during Sunday service. I decided to smile at her and speak every time I saw her. I tried to make small talk about my kids, her kids, the service—anything!

I don't really remember when it changed, but what I will never forget is the day she came to me with a gift of friendship.

The choir was singing one of my favorite selections. As the words and music danced in my spirit, I felt a sharp point tap me on the arm. Vanessa was passing me a card in a sealed envelope. "Read later" was written on the front. I quickly tucked it in my Bible and continued to enjoy the praise and worship service.

After the service she hugged me. Later, I remembered the card and opened it. The words took my breath away as I read, "Out of all the women here, you most reflect a godly woman."

In the weeks to come, we would share many warm greetings, but none so heart-stopping as that first greeting card she gave me. I never learned what happened that changed our relationship. But she once told me that no matter how ungodly she acted toward me, I still treated her in a godly manner.

I feel God allowed me to withstand the hurts Vanessa caused in that time period to grow me in my peace walk, while at the same time he let her see a model of someone trying to have Christ's peace ruling in the heart.

Hurtful situations and pain enter all our lives. I've learned that as we desire to become more and more like Christ, we can take the hurts others cause, place them in the rinse cycle of forgiveness, squeeze out the pain, and allow the peace of Christ to soften our hearts. This enables us to bear with others and walk in peace.

—Sheila Farmer

CHANGING TABLES . . .
CHANGING HEARTS

My rocking chair creaked as I cried out to no one in particular. "It's not fair," I protested. "I just don't understand!"

I was aware that God heard me, although I didn't have the courage to speak the words directly to him. Burning tears rolled down my cheeks and splashed onto my very pregnant front.

Two thousand miles from family, pregnant with our third child, and struggling to adapt to our cross-country move to a better job for my husband, I had many reasons to hope and much to look forward to. But my "heart's eye" saw only our struggle as a one-income family. I continually wondered if I should get a job to take some pressure off our tight budget, but that had not been in our plans.

We already had two sons, and we hoped for a girl this time. White eyelet curtains and a beautiful, white, Jenny Lind crib waited in the third bedroom. We had never before had an extra room for a nursery, and we lacked only the piece of furniture that had caused my tears—a white wooden changing table.

I had seen it in a nearby furniture store and visualized how perfectly it would fit in the nursery. Besides, it was practical: I needed storage space, and it would prevent me from straining my back while changing diapers. I had figured just the right approach to make it impossible for my husband to refuse my request.

That evening I mentally rehearsed my speech as I waited for the right time to make my appeal. After dinner and the children's bedtime, the perfect moment arrived. Carefully—perhaps even a bit manipulatively—I explained the need for this coveted purchase.

As he listened, my husband's furrowed brow and tense shoulders did not communicate what I expected. He sighed and slowly answered, "Honey, it isn't possible right now to buy something like that."

Hadn't he understood? Had I said the wrong thing? Didn't he care about my health, about what would make it easier for me to be home with three children?

Weeks went by, and I continued to pout about the changing table—and one really can pout when pregnant! Didn't God care about my disappointment? Wasn't it in his power to provide what I needed—such a small thing?

Maybe we could stretch a few dollars. Maybe after the baby arrived, we could manage the purchase. I studied every angle in my mind but met defeat each time a paycheck came . . . and went. My stubborn heart refused to understand that the Lord would take care of me even in the smallest details. What should have been a growing trust in God was twisting into an ugly, selfish demand.

A few days later, on my way to the grocery store, driving down a street I didn't usually travel, I saw it! Perched on someone's lawn, among the assorted yard-sale items, was a white wooden changing table! It wasn't the exact table I had seen, but it was beautiful.

I screeched to a halt at the curb. My hand trembled as I unfolded my nine-months-pregnant body from the car and approached the beautiful white vision.

A lady cheerfully asked if she could help me. "How much do you want for the changing table?" I stammered, not taking my eyes away from it.

"Oh, I'm sorry. It's sold," she answered. "The buyer will pick it up later. He had to get a van to move it."

Sold! Surely not, I thought. Why would God allow me to drive down this street at this particular time and see the coveted prize sitting right in front of me—only for me to learn that it was sold?

I tried to regain my composure as tears welled in my eyes. "How much did it cost?" I asked, telling myself, *I might as well know the whole, bitter truth.*

"I sold it to a man for ten dollars," the woman sympathetically answered, understanding my disappointment. "He paid me and will return for it tomorrow."

Fumbling, I wrote my phone number on a scrap of paper and asked her to call me if the man didn't return. She took the number, but I could tell she didn't hold much hope of using it. I drove home forgetting the grocery trip.

As I walked into the house, depression and disappointment engulfed me. Tears broke loose, and I paced up and down throwing "whys" at God like a one-sided tennis match. Finally, exhausted and relinquishing my demands, I blurted, "I give up! OK, God, please make me willing to forget the table and trust that you have a better plan in mind. I don't understand, but I surrender to you. Please forgive my demands and lack of trust, and please cleanse my heart."

When the following weekend arrived without a phone

call, I knew the table must be gone. I fought the blue mood that attempted to raise its ugly head. "Oh, God, I'm willing to be willing, but I need your help," I prayed.

I searched for something productive on which to focus my energy. The nursery closet needed to be cleaned out, so I set to work.

The following morning, the phone call surprised me. "Do you still want the changing table? The man never showed up to get it, and we leave in a few minutes. The moving van is pulling out. If you still want it, come and get it."

My mind spun. "Do you want cash? I could come as soon as I go by the bank."

"No," came the reply. "The man paid me and never came back to collect his money or the table. We're leaving, and the table is on the curb. The garbage man gets it if you don't. I just wanted to let you know that you could have it if you still want it."

"Oh, thank you," I stammered. I gripped the phone in disbelief. Tears came again as I spoke aloud to God. "Oh, Lord, I've been so ungrateful! You didn't want me to buy a changing table. You wanted to give me one! Thank you for being patient and for teaching me more about trusting you. I'm sorry I questioned you."

I grabbed my car keys and sped to the house before someone else collected my abandoned treasure. A Scripture echoed through my mind as I drove away: *"I know the plans I have for you," says the LORD. "They are plans for good and not for disaster, to give you a future and a hope. In those days when you pray, I will listen. If you look for me wholeheartedly, you will find me"* (Jeremiah 29:11-13).

Through this experience, God did teach me that I could

trust him—even in small things. In the years that followed, we would train our children, later homeschool them, and look back at the bountiful and merciful grace that he gave for the task. He gave me much more than a changing table; he gave me a changed heart.

—Marilyn Rockett

ANGEL EYES

Have you ever had an encounter with a complete stranger and afterward come to the near-certain belief an angel has paid you a visit?

You know the kind of angel I'm talking about: one who masquerades as a homeless person during the Christmas season, let's say, on a mission from God to get some selfish Scrooge to recognize his own good fortune long enough to share the wealth.

The day I met my angel, I had slept only four hours, following a twenty-four-hour bout of wakefulness, and I had to go out in public. But the public I had to go out into was a so-so public. I figured it didn't matter if I wore my almost-a-bag-lady barn coat and had two major zits I hadn't concealed with makeup. Because I was wearing a purple sweater and brown socks, I also figured it didn't much matter that I sported a case of bed-head which was anything but sporty.

I only needed to run down to a crummy gas station near the interstate to get my car inspected. It would take ten minutes, and I'd fork over twelve bucks before heading home for a long winter's nap. I was sure I wouldn't see anybody I knew.

I was right. I didn't see anyone I knew. But it wasn't a ten-minute stop, either. My car needed three hours' worth of work to pass inspection. I decided to wait it out at the shop.

If an angel had volunteered to take my place on the greasy folding chair in the tiny waiting area and to call me when the whole unsavory ordeal had ended, I would have kissed her feet.

But what kind of an angel would volunteer a stint in a joint like this? One of those fake-homeless angels like Roma Downey, maybe, strung out on too many overcaffeinated espressos?

Toward the end of my wait, a young girl came in to get her car inspected. She cast a not-too-trusting look in my direction, must have decided my questionable company was better than none, and sat next to me.

We talked about the weather before we moved on—first to her upbringing in Iowa and then to her recent move to Kansas City. We talked about college, and how her new husband had quit after two years to join the military.

"He left for Iraq the week before Thanksgiving," she said. "I can't even turn on the news, I'm so upset. I just go to work and try not to think about it."

Then she told me about her job teaching second graders at a small Christian school in an even seedier part of town. I noticed the green magic-marker streak on her sweater and the specks of silver glitter on her shoe.

"Has your husband called home since he's been in Iraq?" I asked.

"No. He called from Kuwait to say he was on his way to Iraq, but I haven't heard anything since he's been there. I don't even know where in Iraq he is. Besides, it's so expensive to call. . . ."

Do you ever look for angels in daily life? I don't often, I must admit. But the Bible gives every indication I may have been in the presence of them—and may have even seen them without realizing their identity—on any number of occasions.

Somehow, though, this girl—with the runs in her black stockings stopped with clear nail polish and her fresh-scrubbed face—looked just like an angel to me, a wistful, lonely young angel hungry for a word from the man she'd joined her life with such a short time earlier. I remembered those early days of my own marriage—the desperate longing to be together all the time, the eternal issue of outgo surpassing income.

Jesus said that people who share a cup of cold water with a thirsty soul have a reward waiting in heaven. But what about sharing the sound of a ringing phone where a loved one waited in silence? Wouldn't that quench the lonely heart's thirst as surely as water relieves a parched throat?

They called her name after only ten minutes. I watched as she drew twelve one-dollar bills from her purse and laid them individually on the counter, as if the drawn-out process would somehow make them last longer. She thanked the attendant and turned to leave.

She beamed a radiant smile in my direction.

"Merry Christmas," she said, reaching for my hand.

Are pretty young angels really surprised when mere mortals press a wad of cash into their open palms?

"Buy your husband a calling card," I said. "Tell him it's from a weird old gal you met at the gas station. That'll keep him guessing."

She took the money and embraced me, promising to send him the card. He'll call home soon. I'm sure of it. Who wouldn't call, knowing an angel waited on the other end?

She left the station, and as she walked toward her car,

she turned and flashed me another big grin. But this time, there was something like a flicker of recognition in her eyes.

Yesterday, I looked—and felt—like a human being in desperate need of her own personal angel.

Today, a lonely girl in Kansas City thinks a bag lady may have been one.

—Katy McKenna Raymond

GRANDMOTHER'S LEGACY
VIA MY COMPUTER

The bleak, dreary weather matched the miserable mood I'd wallowed in for a week. I let out a long groan. Lying across my unmade bed, I listened for a "What's wrong, honey?"

When there was no response, I remembered that my husband had left earlier to work out at the gym, so with no one around to appreciate my misery, I dressed.

Last week, when I was still only sixty-nine years old, I felt fine; but suddenly the age seventy whispered, "You poor dear; there's so little time left to accomplish all the dreams on your 'To Do' list!"

I much preferred moping around in my bathrobe, but using every ounce of my waning strength, I slowly pulled on the bright yellow slacks I had received for my birthday and wondered how long it would take me to learn to walk at a slow shuffle now that I'm so old.

A voice from my childhood echoed in my head—*Idle hands are the devil's workshop*—so with one more groan, I put on a snappy black-and-white striped shirt with bright flowers scattered across the top, ran a brush through my short white hair, and went to the computer room for something to do.

No way would I open e-mails, because my in-box would be full of those disgusting birthday jokes about the "fun" of old age, so this was the day to back up several years of family photograph files just hanging out in my computer. I carefully labeled a fancy new memory key that would hold tons of stuff, plugged it into the proper slot on my CPU, and got started.

Wow! I thought. *This is great. I shouldn't have put it off so long.*

Things went well, and to say I felt smug is grossly understating the self-pride that took my mind off old age.

I zipped along, transferring photographs from files to the memory key, when—with no warning, no sirens or bells—three months of prize digital photographs disappeared right before my eyes. My newest great-niece just . . . evaporated. The smiling, glowing image of my twenty-year-old grandson when he changed from a long-haired hippie to a fine-looking young businessman vanished. Erased.

Fighting back tears, I spent two fruitless hours carefully searching the computer. Nothing. Not one snapshot taken in the last three months was in any of my files, folders, or documents. The recycle bin was hopelessly empty. Not one of my priceless pictures had slipped into an archived or zipped file.

I am reasonably competent and computer savvy, but my self-assuredness slid into bleak hopelessness. The longer I searched for my lost photographs, the more I returned to feeling worn out and used up and, in general, defeated. Then the crying started. For real. Between sniffling and blowing, I kept flipping through files to verify that no other photographs were lost.

Because tears blurred my vision, I didn't recognize the skinny, young adults in the faded photograph that popped onto my computer screen. I cleaned my glasses and looked closer. Suddenly, that long-ago day flashed to life. I remembered complaining when someone snapped a picture of our scraggly crew. A bunch of us twenty-something parents had taken our children on a hike across the deep, hot, sand dunes in Monahans, Texas, reaching our chosen summit at high noon. Standing beside us with a self-satisfied smile was my Grandmother Alice. She was the short woman on the left, the sixty-eight-year-old lady who had led the pack!

The photograph, taken with an old Brownie camera and scanned with my modern equipment, had remained safely preserved. I stared at it for a long time. Then, shutting down the computer, I wiped my eyes and shoved my cell phone into my pocket. I needed fresh air and as much distance between modern technological skulduggery and me as possible.

Normally when I need God's special reassurance, I lift my eyes to the hills surrounding our comfortable country home and talk it out with my Father. But my heart was in knots and I was confused and pouting, so I kept my head down and wandered around, absently pulling a weed here, kicking a rock out of the way there. Finally, I sat on the swing under the oak tree, held on for dear life, and simply let the memories flow.

My feisty but precious Grandmother Alice was an adventurous, self-reliant woman who knew without doubt that God walked with her. My granddaddy adored his lively wife, and she came first in his life, right after God, so his primary mission was to help her do anything that popped into her head. She began teaching private kindergarten in their home during World War II, just for the fun of it. I smiled, remembering the little red chair in the corner of my living room. It is the only one left from the dozens of little chairs he made for her students.

Grandmother packed her days to the brim with teaching kindergarten classes, volunteering for the church, gardening, cooking three meals a day for Granddaddy, and looking after military families stationed in our little town during the war.

My mother had her hands full with our home and my little brother because the navy sent my daddy away to war. I was a "big girl" in first grade, but when I felt lost, Grandmother always stopped her busy world, pulled me onto her lap, and sang "Jesus loves me, this I know, for the Bible tells me so . . ." until long after I stopped crying.

My grandparents were soul mates, and when Granddaddy died in 1948, their big house was too quiet without his laughter. The empty rooms echoed in the night, and teaching kindergarten had lost its glitter. It never occurred to my grandmother to fear anything, so when she was widowed at fifty-four, she stepped out into the world of the early 1950s to earn a living. She unknowingly crashed through age and gender barriers ahead of her time.

Grandmother easily landed a sales job traveling alone around the state of Texas as the follow-up person who met with families a couple of weeks after a photographer had taken portraits. She drove her own automobile, before cell phones and automatic door locks, to every little out-of-the-way community in the state. She stayed in seedy hotels, ate in greasy-spoon cafés, and made friends with anyone who happened by, never hesitating to talk about her Lord Jesus. Five days a week, she dressed in her finest, opened her bag of photograph proofs, and turned prospects into buyers.

Selling pictures was a snap for her because she knew the

value of the never-to-return moment the photographer had captured on film. Her "sales pitch" was simply words of truth from the heart of a woman who had been orphaned at three years old and, later, buried an infant son, a twenty-seven-year-old daughter, and a husband. She sold photographs with joy because she understood how to hold life close to the heart.

In those days, being a champion saleswoman made my grandmother a celebrity among her colleagues, so the business owner called a special meeting at the home office, which was in Oregon. Grandmother Alice eagerly climbed into a tiny private airplane that would fly her from Texas to the West Coast and absorbed every sight and sound above and below the little plane. Then, in strange surroundings, she graciously met important executives, received awards, and delivered a speech to a roomful of floundering salesmen. Speaking to those strangers was as easy as talking to the Women's Missionary Union at her home church.

Around her sixtieth birthday, traveling became boring, so among other opportunities she pursued, her favorite was a job that, in her mind, was easy. For several years she was housemother to school-age children in an orphanage. The job came with a new brick house, a lovely campus, and ten children who were alone in the world except for "Mama Alice" and her very big God.

Gliding back and forth on my swing and thinking about the dragons she had slain, my own words came back to me: "Grandmother Alice, you must slow down. After all, you're seventy years old; why don't you live with one of us?"

Her answer bounced off the hills around me: "Young lady, what makes you think God can't take care of me? Didn't

I teach you that Moses was *eighty* years old when God called him to take the children of Israel out of Egypt? Don't you know Abraham's Sarah was older than *ninety-five* when she gave birth to Isaac? What do you want me to do? Just sit down and twiddle my thumbs?"

How different things might have been forty-three years ago if dating or remarriage among senior citizens had been OK, or if there had been life-alert buttons, efficient EMS personnel, knowledge of healthy eating, and senior-citizen activity centers with exercise classes, line dancing, meals-on-wheels, and quilting rooms.

Much sooner than she planned, Grandmother's determination lost out to crippling arthritis. She eventually moved in with my parents and then into a nursing home. Senior-citizen homes had no activity directors in those days—so Grandmother became one. Ignoring debilitating pain and unwilling to sit alone in her room, she taught poetry writing, organized afternoon sing-alongs, and conducted Bible classes.

By the time her worn-out body had endured for eighty-eight years, a final illness was too much. Thankfully, she lingered long enough for me to get to the hospital just before she slipped into a coma. Through the night, I held her hand while I talked and sang to her. As eager as she was to see her Jesus, I didn't understand why she clung to life that night. Toward morning, while I was still talking to her, she sang to me! So, as I sang, "Jesus loves me, this I know, for the Bible tells me so . . . ," her hand let go of mine. She didn't even stop to wave. She just walked into God's presence.

I was stiff from sitting on the wooden swing. Noticing that the dreary weather had cleared, I looked up to the hills.

Grandmother Alice had given me a legacy of strength and determination, and both she and my mother had planted the truth of God's Word in my heart.

I made some big mistakes along my way, but I raised my children in God's Word, taught kindergarten, became a foster parent, and took in my two-year-old grandson to raise when I was in my fifties. I tangled with computers, satellite TV, and digital cameras; I became a published writer; and I directed a senior-citizen activity center before I retired. Since then, I've continued to write, and in my senior years, God surprised me with a soul mate—a new husband.

I have no idea when I became my Grandmother Alice, but I know that God walked every step with me.

Feeling my old/young sixty-nine-year-old self again, I went back to my computer and finished backing up price-less snapshots. Then I clicked on the forty-five-year-old faded picture of our family outing and set it as the desktop image decorating my computer. Of all things, I was sure my young Grandmother Alice winked at me from those hot sand dunes.

—Liz Hoyt Eberle

OUR ARMOR OF GOD

Sunlight peeked around the bedroom curtain, teasing me. I shook my head. It seemed wrong for such a beautiful day to bring so much misery into our lives.

I moved into the bathroom, fastening on a necklace. I fingered the cross dangling from the chain. So dainty, yet symbolizing so much might—the power of the cross.

My husband and I locked eyes in the mirror. His eyes reflected stress and worry. My heart twisted. The past three years had taken their toll on us both as we spent—and wasted—time and energy. We knew this day would eventually come; we had known it from the moment the indictment had been handed down. Someone in my husband's office had been accused of illegal procedures, and everyone in middle management and above had been slapped with indictments. So now we faced our day in court for my husband's trial.

"Do I look all right?" His voice cracked with the question. He buttoned and unbuttoned his jacket. It was a nervous quirk, but endearing to me.

Instead of giving him a pat, you-look-fine-dear answer, I studied him, really taking in every aspect of his appearance, although I knew each feature by memory. My husband is a tall man, six feet four inches to be exact. He has dark hair with a generous mix of gray, mainly at his temples. His hazel eyes are flecked with gold around the iris. But I noticed none of that. Not this morning. I stared at his forehead, once smooth but now creased. The slick spot on his forehead where I'd anointed him with oil earlier glistened under the unforgiving bathroom lights. The Windsor knot in his red tie—the color our attorney had instructed him to wear every day of the trial—was snuggled against his neck. The tie matched the other four hanging in the closet, still with the tags attached.

My gaze drifted over my beloved's wide shoulders, made more pronounced by the new gray suit jacket. This was a suit we didn't have the money to purchase, but our attorney had demanded we have. I smiled. A friend who'd never met my husband had heard of our dilemma and delivered funds for a new suit "on her." As he smoothed the sleeves, I knew my friend would be awake and praying for us.

So many of my friends would be fasting and covering us in prayer today. I could feel them knocking on the door to the throne room already, and it wasn't even eight yet.

Refusing to get sidetracked, I continued my assessment. The buckle of his belt shone, tight and sturdy around his waist, the center of his being. Just this morning, I'd prayed over that belt, that God's strength and peace would surround my husband as firmly and surely as the leather.

I dropped my scrutiny to his hips. His front right pocket held a handkerchief. I couldn't see it, but I knew it was there. My sisters and brother-in-law had sent ten handkerchiefs to remind us they were praying for peace and reassurance of God's promises. I had a matching one in my skirt pocket; I slipped my hand inside and touched the smooth cotton. Comfort seeped into my heart.

I shifted my focus downward to my husband's feet, encased inside his stiff dress shoes. I'd prayed that those shoes would help him walk in the Spirit throughout this whole ordeal. For a moment, my mind wandered. *How had I never noticed that the words* ordeal *and* trial *were almost interchangeable?* I'd never forget the parallel from this day forward.

"Babe? You OK?"

I lifted my gaze to his face—the face I'd loved for nearly two decades, the face that had smiled as each of our three daughters was brought into this world, the face I sought out each time a disappointment threatened to destroy my dreams or when a hope failed and nearly drowned me. This was the face of my best friend—the man God had sent to walk beside me for my time on earth, the face of the person I loved more now than the day I'd said, "I do."

Smiling, I nodded. "I'm great."

He held out his hand. His palm rested warm against mine. We slowly descended the stairs, side by side. Words weren't needed just now. We had to see the children off to school, reassure my parents everything would be fine, and then head to the courthouse.

We drove in silence—not the awkward I-don't-know-what-to-say silence, but the quietness that stems from love and comfort, feeling each other's heart without having to say a word.

I prayed during the twenty-minute trip. Some might find it odd that I didn't pray for the outcome we so desperately wanted—no, needed. I worshiped. I praised. I thanked. I shed tears.

When we found a parking place and fed the meter, peace found me. I squared my shoulders as we met our attorney. He studied our faces, hard, as if to gauge our emotions.

I smiled at him, and then winked at my husband. We were ready.

The three of us walked through security at the courthouse. I managed to joke with the guard, making him chuckle. We slipped into one of the vacant elevator cars. Inside, a mixture of too many colognes assaulted my senses. I refused to gag. The door slid open, and we strode down the hall. Each step punched my stomach. I shoved my hand into my pocket, feeling the handkerchief, and I offered up another whispered prayer.

I squeezed my husband's hand as we entered the courtroom. Somehow television courtroom dramas don't convey the tension that was hanging in the air. A shroud of uncertainty hung over the Department of Justice seal displayed behind the judge's bench.

The Assistant U.S. Attorney, along with his staff seated at the prosecution's table, turned to stare. It seemed that the F.B.I. agents all but sneered. I felt the heat move all the way up my spine.

My husband squeezed my hand. I focused on him, staring into his eyes until I felt I could see his soul.

I whispered to him, "I never answered your question earlier."

He wore a confused expression, much like our cats look when we hide their ball of string. "What question?"

"You asked if you looked all right."

Unease spread across his face. "Do I?"

"No, you don't look all right."

His eyes widened. "What?"

"You, sweetheart, look better than 'all right.' You look blessed." My voice caught, but I kept going. "From the red tie to the jacket, from the belt to the handkerchief to the shoes, you look blessed. Fully and completely blessed—clothed in the whole armor of God."

Moisture filled his eyes, and I squeezed his hand. I smiled. He knew.

The outcome of this trial didn't matter. Nothing else mattered at all. God was in control. Our heavenly Father would bring us victory.

Our job was simply to believe.

And we did.

—Robin Caroll

MY HEART'S DESIRE

"So, are you going to tell me your heart's desire?" my husband, Gary, asked as he met me at the back door.

"Sure, I made a list of scenic places I want to see," I said. "They aren't too far off your chosen route, but hon, there's something I desire more than anything."

The day before, my husband of forty-two years had repeated his actions of all the other trips we had planned. He laid a paper on my desk. "Here's the proposed trip. What do you think?"

No big surprise, typical action, but this time for some reason I felt miffed that he hadn't discussed the route with me before making the plans.

I skimmed the itinerary. "Don't you think this is a bit lopsided?"

The list included a photo shoot, a boxing museum, another photo shoot, the red rock of Arizona, and Monument Valley. "What's in this trip for me?" I asked.

"Oregon family. What more do you want?" The innocence on his face told me the dear man had no clue how selfish I thought his plans were.

"Maybe I want to see something else," I snapped. It sounded childish, even to me.

"Tell me what your ideas are, and we can look at the map again, OK?"

Out of his hearing, I phoned our daughter. "Marcy, your dad asked me what I wanted to see on our vacation. I have no ideas; help me."

"What an opportunity, Mom. If it was me, I'd type 'American castles' into my search engine," she said.

After we finished talking, I surfed the Web to find more than the red rock of Arizona and Utah. In minutes, I found several locations that interested me between our home in Omaha and our family in Oregon. When I found the Rosemount Museum in Pueblo, Colorado, the romantic description of the mansion started a fire inside me.

"Lord, is it silly to want something more than just a drive from here to there? Gary loves to snap photos, but honestly, that bores me," I prayed. I mused over the excitement I felt when I read about a romantic candlelight dinner. I decided I wanted a trip wrapped in romance. I didn't care as much about where we went as I did about our attitudes while we were on the trip. I wanted a second honeymoon—to act like we were in love again.

After forty-two years?

At work, I shared my fairy-tale ideas with a coworker, Dee. "You know the man will never go for the idea," I admitted. "But I'll never know unless I ask, right?"

"Good luck," Dee called when I left for home.

"Where's your list?" The serious man who met me at the door did not look like my knight in shining armor. As he sat at the kitchen table, I handed him the list of places I wanted to visit.

"There is something that isn't written down," I added

as I sat in his lap. "After forty-two years of marriage, I want romance," I whispered in his ear.

Silence.

"Mook," he said, using the nickname he has for me, "I'm too old."

"Hon, I'm not asking for sex. I want romance," I explained as I nibbled on his ear.

The shock of my request left my excited-about-vacation husband perplexed.

"Romance? Good thing you told me now," he finally sputtered. "I have three months to practice."

I smooched the man.

"These aren't too far away from your proposed plan. See . . ." I watched him read down my list. Lunch at Rosemount Museum in Pueblo, Colorado, a kiss in the middle of the Four Corners Monument, a drive on Route 66, a visit to see the Winchester Mystery House in Southern California, and a stop by some friends' home on our way north to see the Oregon family. I nibbled on his ear again and said, "More than anything, I desire romance. A photographed kiss at every location."

Gary said little about my ideas.

The next night, we met at the dinner table with a map. Very businesslike, my husband drew up plans. He never mentioned romance. I kept the twinkle in my eye and my desires to myself.

By the third night, the trip route looked solidified.

The fourth day, the phone calls started. Gary called me on his break, "Mook, this is your Luke." OK, he was using our old nicknames. Good sign. "I've been telling them here at work that I've got to get in practice. I keep asking, 'What is romance?' Haven't got too many answers yet, but I want you to know I'm working on it."

For three months, the phone calls, love notes, and whispered sweet nothings continued. Gary kissed me in the checkout line at Wal-Mart and impressed the clerks with his promises of a romantic trip.

To fill our campfire evenings, I searched for a traveler's chess set. When I found one at a toy store, I told the teenagers behind the counter about my "heart's desires." They giggled.

"That's so lovely. So romantic. I want your kind of marriage," the cute blonde said as she smiled at me and bagged my purchase. "Come back and tell us about your trip," she invited. My nonsense opened a door to tell the young lady how the Lord had blessed our marriage.

Our budget allowed for gas, a few meals out, a motel in case of rain, and the price of museums. We carried our bed with us—a pickup bed with an inflatable mattress, bedding, and tarps in case we got caught in the rain.

We left home before dawn on my sixtieth birthday. Gary promised me the romantic lunch I had asked for in the antiquated Rosemount Museum.

It didn't happen.

The mansion no longer served lunches. It didn't matter. I enjoyed the tour of the historical buildings, and even more, I loved my husband's efforts to give me the desires of my heart.

Every day of our trip, Gary delighted me. He opened doors for me, kissed me in restaurants, and whispered sweet nothings in my ear. He sang to me, bought me jewelry, stirred up our courtship memories, and created more.

He bought flowers, picked flowers, and reminded me of flowers he'd given me years before. He found eateries, stopped when I chose to snap a picture, and taught me how to frame a photo.

Because of our romantic nonsense, we shared our adventure with total strangers. We discovered this was an open door to share God, who had kept us married through the good and the lean years. We talked with young couples and seniors. We asked those strangers to snap our photos.

One night when we slept in our pickup bed, the sun disappeared before we were ready for sleep. We played chess by flashlight. I'm sure Gary's most chivalrous self let me win. The rest of the evening is a mere memory between childhood sweethearts.

This year we celebrated our forty-eighth anniversary. Gary still turns on the charm and often becomes my knight in shining armor. Then he asks, "Do I give you your heart's desire?"

Our bodies and life situations may change, but I'm so glad we're never too old and will never be married too long for romance.

—Katherine J. Crawford

WHAT I WANT TO BE WHEN I GROW UP

I was in the locker room cleaning up after a quick swim when I heard someone say, "You moved pretty fast in that water."

Glancing around, I spotted an elderly woman in a blue bathing suit. A small puddle of water collected beneath her as she rubbed a towel through her damp, gray hair. She had more wrinkles than a cotton shirt, and they all crinkled into a smile warm enough to melt taffy.

"Thank you," I said, nodding my appreciation. "I saw you swimming in the lane next to mine. You've got a smooth stroke too."

"I work out almost every day," she said. "I like to stay active."

Normally, I wouldn't connect the words *wrinkles* and *gray hair* with the words *work out* and *active*.

"Excuse me for asking," I said, "but how old are you?"

A mischievous light danced in her eyes. "I'm seventy-five years old."

I'm sure my jaw dropped, because she chuckled.

"I play ball, too," she continued, pulling a basketball out of her gym bag. "I'm in a tournament this weekend. I think I'll shoot a few hoops before I leave. Do you play?"

"No," I croaked. "So you're on a team?"

"Oh yes." She shrugged, as if it were no big deal for someone who looked as old as Santa Claus to sprint up and down the court doing layups.

"Wow, I'm impressed," I said. "I want to be like you when I grow up."

That was my first conversation with Shirley. I later discovered she also regularly played tennis, helped organize vacation Bible school at her church, and drove a funky Volkswagen bug. Her pace may have slowed some with age, but Shirley demonstrated that some things—like enthusiasm and joy—don't fade with age.

Shirley isn't the only inspiring girl I know. Last fall I met a ten-year-old soccer player named Stephanie. Competitive and determined, she tore up the field with her athletic speed and agility. She looked as lean as a whisker and stood only as tall as my chest.

Even so, Stephanie had one of the biggest hearts a kid could have. She was too modest to admit her sweet side; I found it out when I was talking with her mother about our children's upcoming birthdays.

"How are you celebrating Stephanie's special day?" I asked.

"She invited all her friends to a party," her mom said. "We'll play a bunch of games and eat cake."

I chuckled, remembering the giggling, squealing squad of girls that attended my daughter's last pool party. "Typical. What does she want?"

Perhaps knowing her next words would shock me, her mom spoke slowly. "Stephanie doesn't want any gifts. She asked her guests to bring donations to benefit a local charity."

"You're kidding," I gasped.

"It's true," her mom said. "Stephanie started that tradition years ago, and so far she has helped the Humane Society and the homeless shelter, as well as other needy organizations."

I listened wide eyed as her mom told me how, as Stephanie's birthday approaches, she explores various local charities and chooses a different one to help each year.

I shook my head in amazement. "You know what?" I said. "I want to be like Stephanie when I grow up."

I don't know many kids who would give up their presents to help someone they've never met. Stephanie may not be tall enough to reach the top of a bookcase, but she demonstrated that no matter what your size, you can reach someone's tallest needs.

I met another extraordinary woman in a small Nebraska town, a writer named Carolyn.

At first glance, Carolyn didn't strike me as being particularly sturdy. Arthritis had crippled her, twisting her fingers and joints in excruciating ways. And her petite frame, thin arms, and disarming smile made her seem like a china doll. In fact, she appeared so delicate, my first inclination was to dote on her.

Carolyn would have none of that. She was as tough as tanned leather baked five years in the sun and had a mind as sharp as a scorpion's tail. She told me one day, "When I was young, I'd face down any number of people, especially if I thought they were wrong. I was more of a precocious tomboy than anything else."

And then tragedy struck, robbing Carolyn of her strength and health . . . but not of her courage and certainly not of her hope. Although she endured several painful surgeries and encountered many frustrating challenges, she faced each one head on.

Today, even with her limited mobility, Carolyn is a force to reckon with. She's an active leader in the community, heading church, library, and other committees. She writes, speaks, teaches, and mentors—and she does it all with great patience, wit, and passion.

After our first encounter, I knew I wanted to be like her, too, when I grew up. Despite her physical boundaries, Carolyn demonstrated that as you use whatever resources you have, there are no boundaries to the positive impact you can make.

Sometimes I feel insignificant compared to the outstanding people I know. I suspect I'm not alone in this. Aren't we all surrounded by women we long to emulate?

Women role models stand out—for example, Roxanne, who raised and homeschooled five children; Marilyn, who started a gym program for preschoolers; Marge, who worked the night shift so she could stay at home with her children during the day; Sandy, who became a leader in a male-dominated company; Anne, who secured a technology grant for her school; Linda, who maintained her integrity while acting with an improvisational comedy team; and Joy, who handled the bookkeeping for her husband's business.

The list could go on and on. These women are intimidating.

But something happened the other day that made me rethink this whole role-model deal.

After spending a rather uneventful weekend with my children—a weekend filled with chores and errands, board games and reading—my daughter plopped next to me on the couch. Holding my face between her slender fingers, she fixed me with a blue-eyed stare.

"Mommy," she said, "I want to be just like you when I grow up."

I think my heart skipped a beat.

At first, I tried to brush off her comment. After all, I didn't feel like a strong example to follow. I'm just an ordinary mom, doing the best I can to take care of my family and keep the house clean—and not always doing such a good job at either one!

"Me?" I said. "You're smart and clever and funny—you could do whatever you set your mind on. Why would you want to be like me?"

She snuggled into my arms and laid her head on my chest. "Because you love me," she murmured. "And I love you, Mommy."

The simplicity of her answer brought tears to my eyes. Love! Of course! How could anyone not be transformed by love? Love is not limited by age, size, or circumstance. Love radiates unfading joy, compassion, courage, and hope. In my life, if I accomplish nothing else but this—loving my children—then I have done the greatest thing!

Every day, we mothers have someone looking up to us with admiration. We might view our contributions to the world as trivial, but those seemingly trivial contributions mean the world to those under our care.

Move over, all you heroic ladies. You've got company. And her name is Mom.

—Lori Z. Scott

CHOOSING OUR PATH

Bob took a sip of coffee and then spoke. "We have three choices. All of them sound good."

For four years, we had lived in Florida while my husband, Bob, worked at Cape Canaveral in the space program. He had helped put a man on the moon and get Apollo 13 home. However, the space program was cutting back, and many NASA employees faced unemployment. We were among the fortunate few who had the option of a transfer.

We sat at the kitchen table and discussed the different places he could choose.

"The first is Rochester, Maine."

I shifted in my chair and said, "The summers in Maine are wonderful. It is a beautiful state, and I would love it in the summertime. The winters, unfortunately, are not to my liking." I was not sure I could stand a Maine winter. I liked the warm weather of Florida. When we were back home in Kansas—which was warmer than Maine—the winters were cold enough for me.

"OK, forget about Maine. Our second choice is Houston, Texas."

What was not to like about Texas? I went to college in Texas. Houston was on the Gulf and offered warm weather year round. It was also closer to Kansas. But because both of us were from a small rural area in Kansas, the hustle and bustle of Houston brought doubts about living in a big city.

"Why can't they put a space facility in Kansas?"

Bob laughed and gave me no answer. Our third choice was the most exciting.

"How would you like the Australian outback?"

"Bob, you're kidding. We could have such an adventure!"

We talked for some time on the advantages of Australia. Because I had a Florida teaching certificate, I would be able to homeschool the girls. Our oldest was in second grade, and the middle girl was in first. Our baby girl was just two.

This choice sure looked good. Bob said the company would even move our trailer house from Florida to Australia. His salary would be tax exempt. Mentally, I was ready to go immediately.

"Our biggest problem," Bob said, "is that we will be sixty miles from the nearest town and twenty miles from an Aboriginal village. I'll be gone two weeks of every month checking the tracking stations, and that would leave you and the three girls alone. You could travel with me, but that would be hard on the girls."

This was scary. Being unable to visit family back home was another big point against Australia.

We weighed the pros and cons of each choice and prayed for guidance. Each option had good and bad points. One day we would choose one. "Yes, this is where we should go." The next day we would change our minds.

Above all, we wanted God's direction in the way to go. We prayed about which place was best for the girls. We continued to wait for God's answer.

I kept thinking about Kansas. Four years in Florida had seemed like an eternity; I wanted to go home, but what did God want for our family?

All our extended family was in Kansas. All the grandmas and grandpas, aunts, uncles, and cousins lived in the same area. Our girls would never have the chance to know their relatives if Bob continued in the space program.

NASA had tracking stations all around the world that picked up and recorded information. Many times Bob traveled to the island of Antigua or to South America to check on and repair tracking stations. However, there were no stations in Kansas. We continued to pray.

I kept the thought of going home to myself. Bob loved working in the space program, and I did not want him to feel he had to give up his career. We waited for God's answer because we knew he would show us the right way.

I remembered Psalm 37:5: "Commit everything you do to the LORD. Trust him, and he will help you."

One night, Bob approached me about the move. "I don't want you to be upset, but I don't feel any of these choices are right for us. What would you say if we went home? It would be the best place to raise the girls, and I feel God would have us back in Kansas. I think our parents will need us in the future, and I want the girls to know them."

I was so happy. God had been leading both of us to the path he wanted us to take. We turned down the transfers and went home—a decision we never regretted.

Bob was right. Our parents did need us. The year after we came home, my father-in-law died and Bob's mother needed him to help her close the farm, sell out, and move to town. As my parents and Bob's mother aged, we became the caregivers.

True, we faced harder times financially. We went from a high-paying job to small-town wages, but God always provided. Our three daughters got to know their extended family. They had the opportunity to attend the same church that Bob and I had attended when we were young. The advantages and the disadvantages of a small town were theirs.

God does direct our paths. When we listen and put his will before our wants, we just might get our hearts' desires.

—Carol Russell

KICKBOXING OR CHOCOLATE?

"O-o-o-o-h," I groaned when the twitch of pain hit me. Unfortunately, I knew I'd be in a lot more pain before the next hour was over.

I participate in a weekly kickboxing class at my local fitness center. I had arrived at the gym early and spent a few minutes running and warming up on the treadmill. At that point, I already regretted the fact that I'd missed class the week before. I knew that once I got started in the workout room, I'd feel the pain ten times more than if I'd been a good girl and not missed a session!

As I continued to jog on the treadmill, I debated whether or not to just go home and forget the whole thing. I was already in a bad mood—I felt incredibly sleepy; I was sore from the workout two days earlier; and I was, overall, just having a "fat day." The thought of going into that classroom already tired and discouraged made me want to go home and eat. Or, honestly, stop at Old Navy first, spend money I didn't have, and *then* go home and eat! Shopping and chocolate sounded much better than sweat and effort!

But for some reason, I didn't go home. Maybe my discipline showed up for once! Maybe I was so tired I was operating on autopilot. Whatever the reason, I got off the treadmill, walked into the classroom, helped set up the punching bags and floor mats, tugged on my gloves, and moved right into the routine.

Thankfully, our kickboxing instructor plays loud music to keep our energy up during the thirty- to sixty-second segments of various moves. First she'll demonstrate a move—sometimes complex, sometimes simple—say "go," turn on the music, and make us do that one move steadily, as fast and as hard as we possibly can, for the full allotted time—usually about a minute. Then it's immediately off to the next set of instructions. Whew!

So, I punched and chopped and kicked and spun and did the very best I could, sweat dripping into my eyes, shoulders trembling, and hands sore. But I was determined not to stop, determined to prove that I could do it, even though I felt like collapsing on the mat and curling into the fetal position. I kept at it, and even earned a few compliments from the instructor. Surprisingly, I ended up doing better on some of the harder kicks than I ever had before.

At the end of the hour, exhausted, soaked, and with muscles shaking uncontrollably, I realized I felt . . . good. Really good! I had done it! I had given myself a great workout, burned calories, proved I had discipline, and didn't feel so heavy anymore. Let's face it—there's no better way to beat a "fat day" than with exercise! (Of course, chocolate helps, too, but only temporarily.) There is something to be said for those endorphins after all!

I stumbled to my car, resembling a limp white noodle, and drove home thinking, *What if I had given up?*

I'd probably have gone to my house, slouched on the couch, watched mindless reruns on TV, eaten something incredibly fattening for dinner, and then regretted it afterward. How much fun would that have been? Instead, I did what I knew I needed to do: I kept myself accountable to the class and to my instructor, completed a successful workout, and even enjoyed myself.

Then a parallel hit me hard. For several weeks, my career had been hitting rough spots. I'd fought doubts and Satan's lies that said, "I'm not good enough," "I misunderstood God's call," "I can't do this!"

The battle was exhausting.

But if I gave up, how much fun would that be? I'd feel worse afterward, just as I would have had I gone home to binge instead of disciplining myself to attend class.

Sometimes, that little word *persistence* can go an awfully long way. As women, we tend to keep our plates full to overflowing, trying to squeeze in enough room for husbands, kids, work, housecleaning, self-image, weight control, hormone control, and more. We rarely have any room for "me time." We're shuffling the kids around, keeping up with the house, checking off an endless list of chores, wishing we had the energy to put our own personal dreams into action.

Needless to say, we often feel like giving up. We might think, *Hey, this isn't what I signed up for!* Or *I'm not good enough.* Other times we say to ourselves, *This is way too hard* or *I'm too tired.*

These thoughts are normal for those of us with goals and dreams we hope to accomplish. But normal doesn't always mean right. Just because every woman has these thoughts at some time or another doesn't make them true! They are lies.

When God calls us to do something, it's our job to go

for it, regardless of the guarantee of success or lack thereof. Regardless of the pain and effort and energy spent. Regardless of the fact that we'd rather hide under the covers with a pint of Ben & Jerry's!

God's timing and ways aren't the same as ours. They're much higher because he sees the big picture. He knows exactly where we're going, while we're stuck with "treadmill vision," feeling as if we're not getting anywhere. Though God doesn't always promise us the exact results we desire, he does guarantee abundant life if we abide in him.

I can attend kickboxing classes for the rest of my life and still not be guaranteed six-pack abs or buns of steel. But I can be sure that I am improving my overall health, learning self-defense, burning calories, and making myself look good.

If we want to accomplish our goal of being fit and healthy, we have to burn away calories, exercise our muscles, and control our eating habits. In the same way, if we want to accomplish our dreams, we have to burn away the fear, exercise our talents, and control our doubts. Sure, it's hard work. It's tiring and often takes more energy than we feel we have to give. But it's more than worth the effort.

And the very best part is . . . we don't have to do it all alone.

Jesus is jogging beside us, wiping our foreheads with a crisp white towel and offering a fresh swig of Living Water. And just when we feel we can't take another step, he leans in close and whispers, "You can do this. I've already provided you with everything you need! Just . . . keep . . . going."

—Betsy Ann St. Amant

BIG, BAD, BUNNY BLESSINGS

What are the job specifications for a classroom rabbit? Perky ears? Twinkly eyes? Sweet disposition? A penchant for nibbling carrots? Nicholas, my classroom bunny, failed on all counts. Perhaps it was due to the fact that she was named Nicholas long before she was discovered to be of the female persuasion. Or maybe giant, lop-eared rabbits are exempt from these sappy requirements. Whatever the case, her ears hung down, and her eyes were frequently narrowed.

Nikki was a big, bad, armful of mischief wearing a fur coat.

She came into my class because something was missing. Sure, the curriculum was packed in tight. Yes, the rules and regulations were firmly in place. But there was one piece missing, which I was not allowed to give my students, and it was the most important piece. In a public school there was to be no talk of God. He would not be a part of the children's lives from eight to three, and if there was any ministering that needed to be done, the words should be couched in safe, sterile, God-free language. Period.

So I delivered on my end of the bargain, hoping that God would find a way into our classroom without my direct instruction. First John 3:18 would be my mantra: "Dear children, let's not merely say that we love each other; let us show the truth by our actions."

Months into the school year, I had not resolved my dilemma. My students knew I cared about them and their academic achievement, but did they know that God adored their precious souls with all the unconditional love of a perfect Father? Suddenly, a brainstorm! Would having something small and helpless to care for give them a taste of that love? Enter Nikki the rabbit.

The day I adopted that naughty nine-month-old, I scooped her up for a tender hug. Who knew a rabbit could execute a perfect double snap kick? Flip the animal on her back and she'll be instantly docile, proclaimed chapter three of my *Your Rabbit and You* book. Sad to say, Nikki had not read the manual. The back-flipping maneuver sent her into a Tasmanian devil fit. At the end, we retreated to our corners, sides heaving, hair mussed. I am sure that rabbit was muttering unflattering things about my parentage.

After many negotiations and a dozen Band-Aids, we reached détente. I wouldn't try to hold her, and she would accept gentle petting and vegetable treats. There would be no flipping, and not too many caresses would be permitted. Should the rabbit require relocation, I was to stand close and herd the animal in the desired direction, whereupon she would or would not acquiesce to my demands. Under no circumstances was there to be any lifting up of said animal.

I communicated these rules to my fifth-grade students when I moved Nikki into our classroom. Her cage fit neatly under the back counter, complete with wooden nesting box, alfalfa hayrack, and two water bottles. She was far enough away so as not to distract the students unless she had a bunny hissy fit and shot around the cage, crashing into the bars and making all manner of noise. I had the sneaking suspicion she did this on purpose.

As a new teacher, I believed in control and discipline. That was the way to keep all hands sailing toward our educational goals—structure, unwavering schedules, every lesson planned in the minutest detail. Even though the animal seemed to model nothing but bad temper, perhaps she could reinforce responsibility and routine, with scheduled times for feeding, a rotating roster of caregivers, and cleaning duties assigned and carried out at regular intervals. The children would be exposed to the animal kingdom in a calm, controlled setting.

Too bad the rabbit had other plans.

There was the time she made a stealthy break through the back door. We assumed she was hanging out in her spot behind the bookcase and didn't think anything of her absence until a stalwart yard-duty monitor brought her back from the playground. Fortunately, no Band-Aids were required for the startled woman as she herded the growling pet back to our room.

Months later I enjoyed a full week of uninterrupted class time before I discovered why—my adorable pet had eaten through the phone line. A helpful clerk at the pet store suggested I paint the cords with Tabasco sauce. However, Nikki apparently was a bunny with a taste for spicy food. She continued to chomp through them with gusto. I bought several replacement cords before I gave up and moved the phone to the top of a rolling cabinet. My well-trained phone monitors learned to pull up a stepladder when they needed to field a call.

It was time to admit defeat. The pet experiment was a failure. I had decided to take her back home to live out her days in my backyard, until I noticed an interesting phenomenon. The kids had grown to love that rabbit with a passion. They doted on the old grouch. She was mean and crabby and fickle . . . and they loved her. They showed it with their deeds a hundred times a day. The lucky pet monitor enjoyed the privilege of feeding her, filling her bottle, and sitting next to her favorite haunt during silent reading time. If the children became overly attentive, Nikki would inform them of their transgression with a snort, ears flapping in indignation, and hop away. During study time the kids would keep their eyes on their books, while giving the rabbit under their desk a gentle rub with their feet.

Against all good sense, Nikki demonstrated another love lesson. Our school was home to a special day class for children with both physical and emotional problems. Every day after lunch, the teachers would walk these students past our door on their way back to class. One day, I left the door open to catch a cool breeze while the children read silently.

We all looked up at a squeal from the back of the room. Who was throwing a monkey wrench in my sacred quiet period? A little boy with serious emotional difficulties had broken rank from his class and dashed into our room, dropping to his knees to stare at the rabbit.

I held my breath as he plunged a hand into her cage, praying Nikki wouldn't bite him. To my complete astonishment, she sat quietly in her cage, patiently enduring his not-so-gentle pats. The teacher rounded up her errant student, apologizing for the interruption.

That impromptu visit became the beginning of a therapeutic routine for the boy. If he could make it through the morning without major incident, the teacher would allow him to stop in our classroom on the way back from lunch to visit Nikki. He relished those moments with her, and my students and I got to the point where the visits were a regular part of the day. We all learned to expect the exclamations and loud comments from the delighted child, and true to their training, the kids continued with their silent reading, smiling occasionally at the squeals from our visitor.

Over the course of the school year, this wild rabbit—unpredictable, contrary, and petulant—would return from her wanderings and hop back into her cage to be there for the boy's visits. She would flop down on her side at the appointed hour, face pointed toward the door, waiting for her guest to arrive.

She never growled.

She never bit.

She never hopped away from his clumsy petting.

I don't know how she knew, but somehow she saw in that child, and in all my children, people in need of unconditional love. And Nikki, bless her cranky old heart, turned out to be just the rabbit to share it with them. All my lessons, discussions, and lectures didn't amount to one particle of what they learned from Nikki. True, I hadn't brought God into our classroom with my words or actions, but he'd come in nonetheless, in deed and truth, the best Teacher those kids had ever had.

Nikki served many more years in the classroom before I retired her to a quiet spot in a shady corner of my yard. When I found her one day, silent and still, I held her close as I had always wanted to do, and I whispered my thanks in her ear.

And then I thanked God for sharing his big, bad, bunny with me.

—Dana Mentink

PLANTING GOD'S SEEDS

"Your flowers are gorgeous!" the stranger said with a smile as she walked past our driveway with her two dogs in tow.

"Thank you," replied my mother. "I've been working on them all spring. I'm just glad the deer haven't eaten them yet."

"I've discovered a little secret for keeping deer off mine . . ." the stranger's voice trailed off as I walked back inside the house. I'd been helping my mom water her garden.

Ninety degrees in the shade today, and she's out there playing in the dirt, I thought, amused. But I knew there was no place she'd rather be.

She had always tried to get me to help her with the yard and the garden, but I wanted no part of it. After all, why would a teenager want to dig in the dirt with her mother when she could be out playing tennis or riding her bike? I used to think my mom just didn't understand that, because no matter how many times I declined her offer, she'd always ask again the next time she wanted to work in the garden. Eventually I figured out that she wasn't really after my help but rather my company.

I stood inconspicuously at the living room window watching my mom chat with the lady in the driveway. After several moments, the pair headed to the backyard.

What does she find to talk about with a perfect stranger?
I wondered, envious of her extroverted nature. This was
something she and I definitely never shared!

"And these are my favorites." I heard my mother's voice
trickle through the kitchen window. "They come up so beautifully every year. I especially love them because purple is my
favorite color."

After about an hour, they were on the patio, sipping iced
tea. My mom had even filled a bowl of water for the woman's dogs! Before long, my mother's Bible was open and she
was sharing God's Word with her new friend, whose name,
I learned, was Linda. When Linda finally left, she was carrying
a bag—filled with books about Christianity and gardening.

How does she do it? I asked myself.

My mom had led me into a relationship with Christ only
a year before. Though I had a tremendous zeal for God, I
couldn't articulate it well to others. I was amazed at how easy
it was for her to talk about him. I had witnessed this same
scenario time and time again with her and our neighbors. It
was as though she and God had designed a strategy together:
"OK, God, you give me some beautiful flowers to enjoy, and
I'll talk to anyone you send my way."

I can just hear her now, discussing her terms with him.
Because, after all, that is how she talked to God—just like they
were best friends.

"Hey, Jo-Ann!" shouted the neighbor from across the
street. "What kind of fertilizer did you tell me to use on
my azalea bushes?" she asked, walking toward the driveway
where my mom was watering her border annuals. "Oh, and
by the way, I finished that book you gave me. Being raised in
a Jewish home, I've never seen the Old Testament the way

that book talked about it. I'd really like to discuss it with you sometime."

Bam! Just like that. Another open door.

My mother was very frustrated that she didn't have a specific gift or talent. She always wanted to be able to sing or play an instrument. But instead of feeling sorry for herself, she simply made the most of the passions God gave her.

I can still envision her, kneeling in the rich, black soil, meticulously plucking every weed that would dare show itself amidst her flowers. Nearly every day in the springtime as I ran home from the bus stop after school, or in the heat of the summer when I came home from playing in the neighborhood, I'd find my mother somewhere in our yard, tending her garden. Even as a teenager, I found joy in watching her, knowing she was completely in her element. What I didn't fully comprehend was how creatively God was using her for his Kingdom.

For the first few months after Mom met Linda, the two began visiting each other regularly. Linda would walk her dogs past our house, and what started as an impromptu conversation nearly always ended up with them sitting on the porch or patio, laughing and talking like old friends. My mom was typically speckled with soil from head to toe, but she couldn't have cared less. If someone wanted to talk about the Lord, she'd stop whatever she was doing to take advantage of the opportunity.

One day I glanced out the window and saw Linda—this time without her dogs—approach my mother in our yard. My mom hugged her tightly, and they started walking toward the house. As they came closer, I saw that Linda was crying. My mom brought her inside, poured her a cold drink, and began ministering to her.

I left the room so they could talk, and after about an hour, I heard my mom say, "OK, so you and Rick be sure and come over tonight. Seven o'clock. I'll be praying for you."

Linda's husband, Rick, had just been diagnosed with lymphoma. Linda wasted no time telling my mom. She didn't know where else to turn. Our family was having our weekly Bible study that night with some people from our church, and my mom wanted Linda and Rick to come so they could meet others in the faith and be prayed for.

During the next several months, Rick and Linda regularly attended our Bible study. They witnessed God's love in action as group members prayed for them, encouraged them in God's Word, and offered practical assistance whenever they needed help.

"No one ever told me God loved me before," said Linda after one of our meetings. "I knew he loved the world, but I didn't know he loved me personally."

At one of the Bible studies, Rick and Linda gave their hearts to the Lord. Even though Rick's condition deteriorated, they were no longer scared. With Jesus now in their lives, they were able to attain peace—both with Rick's illness and with their eternal destinies.

I remember asking my mother how she made sharing Jesus look so easy and so natural—something I still struggle with today. She said to me, "You probably think I'm just a crazy lady talking to myself in the yard. But I'm actually talking to God. I talk to him about the people he's going to send my way. I ask him to prepare their hearts and make a way for me to speak about him. And I pray for those he's already sent to me, asking him to meet their needs. Then I just have fun with my flowers and stay ready!"

My mother died in December of 2004 at the young age of sixty-three. Linda, who still lived in the neighborhood, was by her side during her final days. My mom probably never fully realized how many people she touched with the love and compassion of Christ and how many she brought close to him—just because she allowed him to use the passion he gave her to reach others.

While she planted her seeds into the soil and patiently removed weeds from her flower beds, God was busy depositing his own seeds and weeding the hearts of those he sent to her. In one important way, my mother was just like her lovely flowers: She bloomed beautifully right where she was planted.

—Renee Gray-Wilburn

WEDDING-GOWN GREASE

Black grease down the front of my wedding dress? LeAnn and I had been friends for years, yet I'd never known her to be a practical joker. It seemed unlike her to tease me this way just an hour before my wedding. When I wiggled into the dress as she held it for me, then looked down at my beautiful white satin gown, I was ready to laugh at her little joke. But like I said, LeAnn had never teased me before. And she wasn't teasing now.

When Richard and I decided to marry, we agreed to have a simple ceremony. As we prepared for marriage, we wanted to focus on our relationship more than on the details of a big wedding. Our decision was also a result of my having been a bridesmaid ten times. Yes, ten times a bridesmaid, and that's not counting the many other jobs I'd done to help make a wedding happen.

When it comes to weddings, I've done it all, and I've seen it all. I've thrown showers; sewn dresses; and baked for, set up, and cleaned up after receptions. I've shopped for gowns, stood by guest books, photographed ceremonies, assisted brides, and chauffeured happy couples. I've also seen how a bride-to-be can lose all sense of rationality. For instance, one dear bride had a major meltdown picking out the color of the stockings her bridesmaids would wear, even though only a few inches of ankle would be visible.

Another bride was so nervous as she dressed for her wedding that she dropped a contact lens in the toilet. Her brother thrust his hands into the toilet to try and retrieve the lens, but to no avail. However, he actually got a replacement lens in time for the ceremony and, to this day, is a hero in his family.

Besides considering how crazed a bride can become when planning the nuptials, she also needs to consider what can go wrong during the event. I've seen brides faint, cakes fall, attendants stumble, and grooms arrive late.

One time, a trucker's CB radio broadcast through the church sound system during the minister's message. At another wedding, someone forgot to prepare for Communion, so Oreos and fruit punch were used.

At one reception, held at a volunteer firehouse, firemen served the meal. It worked out great until the siren blared. All those serving food dropped their utensils, grabbed their coats, and rode off to battle the blaze.

And of course, many couples have gone into debt throwing the wedding of the century, only to later realize they might have spent that money as a down payment on a house.

With such a vast wedding résumé, as well as being a first-time bride at forty-two years of age, I had my eyes wide open to the truth about weddings. They should be a reverent, wonderful celebration where a couple vows before God and others to love each other until death. Instead, weddings sometimes become so overblown and stressful that the couple can't wait for the ceremony to be over. But not me! I was determined to enjoy every moment.

We invited any and all who wanted to come celebrate with us. After the ceremony we would have a simple, chocolate-chip-cookie reception. Then we'd have a much smaller dinner reception at my favorite restaurant for our families. Yep, Richard and I had it all planned. We realized something might go wrong, but it wouldn't matter. By the end of the day, our life together would begin. Our wedding plan was for simple, easy elegance. Richard and his best man would wear tuxedos they already owned. My gorgeous gown was bought off the rack for a modest amount. With satin gloves that went up to the elbows, elegant jewelry, and my hair up, I couldn't have felt more beautiful. My two bridesmaids had stunning dresses from an upscale department store.

So here I was on the big day. LeAnn zipped up my dress. I heard piano music coming from the sanctuary. The air was scented by bouquets of flowers and hundreds of chocolate-chip cookies. And I, the joyous bride, smiled as I looked down to see . . . three long stripes of black grease, half an inch wide and eighteen inches long, down the center of my white satin dress! My taste tends to be simple, so my wedding dress was not decorated with beads, lace, or diamonds, just . . . grease. My head whipped around, looking for the people from *Candid Camera,* only to find four dear girlfriends and my little niece staring at me with startled expressions.

The room was instantly a flurry of activity. During previous predicaments in my life I'd think, *It always makes for a good story later.* But I didn't want a good story, especially not this one!

LeAnn got on her knees with a wet washcloth. As she scrubbed, I took comfort. She was intelligent and kind and had an impressive career in nursing. She knew how to scrub up for surgery in the operating room. Certainly black grease on a white wedding dress was no problem for this superwoman.

After a few minutes of scrubbing, she sat back so we could see the results. Not a smidgen of grease was removed. Now I had *wet* black grease down the front of my dress. In twenty-five minutes we'd begin the preceremony photo session.

My niece began spinning in circles to show how her dress flared out. It was her attempt to distract me. My four dear friends scurried about in another outbreak of activity as I closed my eyes, bargaining with God in prayer. If he took away these black stripes, I wouldn't complain if the cake fell, the cookies crumbled, and the bridesmaids stumbled. I begged forgiveness for any self-centered bridal attitude of which I'd been guilty, and I asked forgiveness for any ungracious thoughts I'd ever had as a bridesmaid.

As I continued reviewing my life (specifically asking forgiveness for the time I didn't want to share my crayons when I was in kindergarten), LeAnn began a new tactic. With a toothbrush and dishwashing detergent, she began working her magic. For thirty minutes she scrubbed and brushed, ignoring her sore knees. The poor thing worked up a sweat toiling over my dress. But it would all be worth it, I was sure. Finally, when she was done, my white wedding gown had three wet, black, grease stains that were guaranteed free of any food particles. We all sighed.

Grease stained or not, it was time for photographs. Mustering my best bridal glow, I started for the door. Maybe if I smiled big enough, no one would notice fifty-four inches of wet black grease on an otherwise perfectly white, size-four wedding gown.

Everyone stood, silent, as I headed for the door.

"Toothpaste!" Lois suddenly bellowed.

We immediately understood. Once more LeAnn was on her knees, this time using her fingers to paint white toothpaste over the grease stripes. Within minutes the stains were hidden under a layer of cavity-fighting paste. There was applause as I twirled in my dress, once again white, but now with tartar control!

My girlfriends left the room so Richard and I could have a few minutes alone. His reaction upon seeing me is a memory I will treasure forever. When I showed him the wet toothpaste-over-grease stripes on my dress, he shook his head. He could see only his beautiful bride. Within minutes, the toothpaste dried perfectly, and no one ever knew there was black grease on my white gown. My stains were covered and forgotten.

What a sweet reminder of Christ's love for us. Our sins are covered by his blood. Because of Christ's love and sacrifice, we can be confident we are loved and beautiful in his eyes. We can share his grace and beauty in this tired, old world. We are loved. We are his.

Just to let you know the end of my story, the cake didn't fall, the cookies didn't crumble, and none of the bridesmaids stumbled. We enjoyed a wonderful celebration of worship, music, and laughter followed by sweet fellowship with family and friends. It truly was a perfect day. And in case you wonder how three stripes of black grease got on my wedding dress, so do I, dear friend . . . so do I.

—Leslie J. Payne

THE LAST STRAW

"I've known a lot of inconsiderate people in my time, but you take the cake!" As I listened to myself scold my coworker in the middle of the office, I was as shocked as he was—and as shocked as our other coworkers, who'd certainly never heard me light into anyone like that. But the situation had started way before that day.

I'd been raised in a small, western Washington logging town, where my parents were loved and respected. I had enjoyed acceptance, approval, and respect from everyone. This increased after I graduated from high school and worked in the school office.

But then Dad passed on, and Mom and I moved to a large city—a whole new world I wasn't prepared for. I'd never been married, and at age thirty-five, I was incredibly naive. I took for granted that Christians who stood by their beliefs and treated others respectfully would be treated the same. Not so. I heard language on the job that no logger would have ever used in my presence.

Through much prayer, I managed to keep my sunny nature and served as an office peacemaker in my new job. Terms such as *lifts morale, positive influence,* and *an asset to the workplace* began to creep into my evaluations. Then I transferred to a new job, as one of only two women in an engineering department that handled maintenance and operations for a government hospital. The men treated me with the same respect I had enjoyed in my hometown.

Only two things marred my new job. One was dealing with a sarcastic second in command. Rick supposedly knew everything. His supercilious attitude antagonized everyone, including me. Despite my irritation, I felt sorry for him. As a coworker said, "It's hard enough for us to be around him. Imagine what it must be like living inside all that misery."

It was misery. Rick's trailer was the size of a big closet. His wife and son lived two hundred miles away. Rick sent her his checks, and she returned just enough money for food. She was having an affair, but Rick hung on for his son's sake. He was physically and morally clean, but straggly hair and unpressed clothing made him unattractive.

The other problem was my silver-haired, married boss. Still naive, I didn't catch on to small, inappropriate remarks until we both worked late one autumn evening. As he walked me to my car, I commented, "It's sure starting to get dark early these days."

He moved closer. "I'll bet it would really be nice to be alone with you in the dark."

I froze, unable to speak.

He sighed and said, "I guess that probably will never happen."

My words dripped icicles. "No. It certainly won't."

Shortly after that, he transferred his unwelcome attentions elsewhere and set off a hospital scandal.

I wanted out. I told God so—again and again. Nothing happened. Just before Christmas, I realized I was no longer the joyous person God wanted me to be. I gave in. "OK, God, I'll stick until you move me. In the meantime, please help me each day."

Weeks passed. Rick grew more and more obnoxious. One of my jobs was to process supply and equipment orders. I had to continually prod Rick to approve the requests, and most were needed immediately.

The straw that broke my self-control came shortly before quitting time on an especially frustrating day. Rick came out of his office and handed me a thick stack of approved requests. "Here you are."

I stared into his smirking face and erupted. "I've known a lot of inconsiderate people in my time, but you take the cake! My other work is caught up, and I've asked you all afternoon for those orders. You only had to take a few minutes to glance over them. Instead, you sat and stared out the window. *Now* you bring them to me? There's no way I can get these done tonight!"

Shaking with fury, I stopped and glanced around the large office. Coworkers stood like statues, mouths hanging open. I knew they were thinking, *This came from Colleen?*

My irrepressible sense of humor took over. I planted my hands on my hips, looked back at Rick, and announced, "I sure told you off. And, boy, do I ever feel better!"

Healing laughter swept through the room. Rick turned and headed for his office. Others returned to their jobs. I just sat there.

I blew it, Lord. What kind of Christian, who's trying to be an example of your Son, dresses down a supervisor, especially in front of a roomful of employees?

I don't recommend spouting like a whale at sea as a good

witnessing tool, but God uses all kinds of situations. From that day on, Rick started a long, slow climb. He approved orders in a timely fashion and always delivered them to my desk. He no longer acted high and mighty. A few weeks later, he overheard me telling someone I was going to get an electrician to install a new wall lamp at home.

"I'm an electrician. I'll do it for you," he volunteered. "Is tonight all right?"

I hid my shock. "Thanks. Do you want to have supper with Mom and me?"

He hesitated. "Won't it put her out?"

"Not at all."

Later that evening, I was clearing the table while Mom visited with Rick in the living room. I realized he must be looking at the picture of Jesus above the mantel because I overheard him say, "I used to have Christ and friends in my life."

Mom quietly told him, "Try out church, Rick. You'll find both."

The next week Rick got his hair cut. He spruced up his clothes and came to church. It was only the beginning. He returned to Christ. He made friends. God had used my outburst as the opening wedge needed to free an imprisoned soul.

Months later I sat on a huge rock beside a rushing stream. Our minister led Rick into the water and said, "I baptize you in the name of the Father, the Son, and the Holy Ghost."

It was a moment of truth for me. The face of the man I had once come close to despising was radiant as he came out of the water. I realized why God hadn't removed me from my unpleasant situation when I begged him to: My work at the hospital hadn't yet been accomplished. That summer God did open the doors to another government agency where I could witness for him. But I did not do it by telling people off!

Rick later became a highly respected minister. He touched many lives over the next years. God truly does work in mysterious ways to perform wonders in the lives of his children.

—Colleen L. Reece

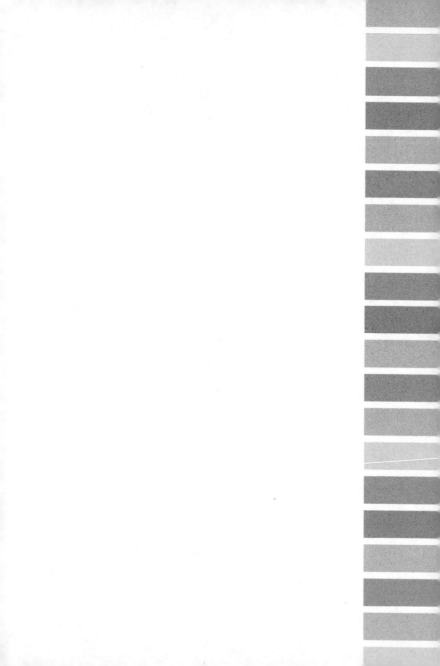

THE NIGHT SHADOW

My heart pumped with fear as I was jolted awake by the Shadow!

I hadn't been asleep very long. My mind had been buzzing with computer jitters after I'd spent hours on e-mail, and I hadn't been able to relax after I'd gone to bed. My husband was out of town and my son was staying with a friend, so I was alone in the quiet house. I'd picked up a mystery novel, entertaining my mind with fictional images of a fantasy world in another time—the Dark Ages.

My mind had finally "de-buzzed" and relaxed, and I'd drifted into la-la land.

But then the Shadow jolted me awake.

Well, I didn't actually see a shadow, although I expected to at any moment. Rather, someone with a very raucous voice was invoking the Shadow, calling for him in the dark pit of night: "Shadow, Shadow, Shadow . . ."

At first, in my half-comatose state, I thought I was dreaming. Worse, I feared that I was about to enter a nightmare and imagined, in my somnolent stupor, that a shadow would appear as if conjured up by a scary sorcerer.

As the voice continued shouting "Shadow," adrenaline surged in my veins and finally shook off my drowsiness. I was not dreaming. Someone outside really was calling, "Shadow, Shadow . . . come here, Shadow!"

The voice started sounding shaky. Upset. And now it was right outside my bedroom window. Some guy was walking up and down our street shouting loudly. Desperately. And I was alone. I hoped I'd locked the door.

He's either high on drugs and thinks he's Peter Pan, I thought, *or he's lost a dog.*

I hoped he'd lost a dog.

So at 3:30 A.M. I prayed, donned myself in bravery, and stuck my head outside the window only to be poked in the face unexpectedly—by a branch from our avocado tree. After whimpering, "Ouch!" I bellowed into the darkness: "Sir, is there a reason you're making so much noise at this hour?"

"Lost my dog," he gruffly answered.

I wasn't bothered that he didn't apologize. I heard the concern in his voice. If that were my dog, I'd be worried too.

"Oh my, I'll be praying," I responded sympathetically.

Although I didn't tell this to the fretting stranger, I'd actually already been praying—for lots of things, including my safety. When I crawled back into bed, I continued praying.

Missing. I recalled the stack of paper I'd pulled out of the mailbox earlier that day. Amid the advertisements and trash was a card with a picture of a four-year-old girl, Acacia, who'd been missing from home since she was one year old. I had immediately prayed for Acacia and for her parents, imagining their torment and sleepless nights.

Such a situation must be unbearable, and I knew that if I were in that position, I'd hope people cared enough to pray. So I chose to pray every time I saw a card with the photo of a missing child.

After remembering Acacia's picture in my mailbox and wondering if the man outside would find Shadow, I finally managed to drift off to sleep again—this time praying for the missing children and a little lost dog.

The next morning after waking, I remembered the events of the night and wondered if the stranger had found his lost pet.

When I walked outside to pick up the mail, I encountered Nora, my neighbor. All five of her bubbly children simultaneously asked if I'd seen a tiny, black dog.

"You mean Shadow?" I asked.

"Oh yes, do you know him? He's our dog, and he ran away last night. We've searched everywhere, but no one's seen him."

I told Nora and her youngsters how I'd heard the cries during the night and had been praying for them to find Shadow.

"I'm sorry about the noise in the night," Nora apologized. "My husband was so anxious to find him. . . . We didn't think about the noise. I hope it didn't disturb you."

"No worry," I quickly replied. "I just prayed and fell back to sleep. Would you like for us to pray for Shadow—that you find him?"

To my surprise, they answered my question with a unanimous "Yes!"

I didn't know if this family even knew Jesus, but my husband and I had prayed for them at different times. Now I had the opportunity to pray *with* them.

So I prayed a quick prayer about the dog, and in my heart I prayed more: *Lord, use this to show them who you are.*

Later that day, Nora told me they'd found Shadow. And

the children told everyone that Jesus did it. God used that little lost dog and my spontaneous prayer to reveal his glory and open a door for me to share more about him to these precious neighbors.

This incident encouraged me to pray more and to be open to the Holy Spirit to boldly pray with unsaved people so that they might see him through us in our prayer. There is so much to pray for, so many situations and people. I am learning to take every situation—every card I get in the mail, every neighbor's problem, and every night shadow—as an opportunity to pray. I am learning to find God at work, even in the Shadows that wake me in the middle of the night.

—Janey DeMeo

On opening night, the atmosphere was electric.

The musicians tuned their instruments as we settled into our seats. These were the best seats we'd ever had, because this time, we had the inside track. We had cast tickets.

My daughter, Lauren, who was ten, was appearing in the local college's spring musical. Forget school plays or Christmas programs, this was the big time. Well, the "big enough" time, anyway.

So, here we were, moments from the lights dimming, and I had the jitters from excitement and anticipation. It was one of those "watching the fledgling take her first flight" moments. I knew she would be terrific, and I couldn't wait for everyone else to see her.

Casually flipping through the program and reading the biographical notes for the cast, I remembered the evening that we'd first read the casting call in the newspaper. We picked up the audition packet, which directed participants to come prepared to perform a song from the musical, perform a song from another Broadway show, read the script, and do a pantomime.

I would have quit at this point. Not Lauren. She bounced out of the performing arts office at the thought of show tunes. We settled on a song from *You're a Good Man, Charlie Brown* for her audition. It was cute, kid-friendly, and familiar: a song she had sung in the backseat of the car a hundred times. Of course, the sheet music was nowhere within a hundred miles of us. Thankfully, there's FedEx.

After a weekend of testing Daddy's sight-reading skills and listening to the show CD over and over, she was as ready as she would ever be. I had no doubt she'd get the part. If they could see in her what I saw every day, it was a slam dunk.

As I drove to the audition, I tried to prepare her, just in case I was wrong. "This is a very subjective business," I said. "Even if you're very good, you may not be what they have in mind."

The audition was open to kids through age fifteen, so it was possible she would be up against girls with more acting and singing experience than she had.

Undaunted, Lauren went into the audition. It was about as intimidating for her as brushing her teeth. She learned the choreography. She sang alone onstage for a group of adults she didn't know, and she read her lines with gusto.

She got a callback, and after the second audition, she was cast in a better part than we expected. Then, for ten weeks I was a "theater mom" as she rehearsed. The final two weeks were intense, especially for a fourth grader—four nights a week for at least three hours—but she was a trooper. And tonight was the payoff.

Finally, the lights dimmed, and the music started. Lauren was in her element. She belonged on that stage. Sure enough, when she skipped on stage in the second act, I was beyond proud. She stood alone in that white-hot spotlight, sang her solo, and delivered her lines with the comedic punch of a pro. Admittedly, I started the applause and was the first one on my feet at the curtain call (Moms are allowed), but she deserved it. At each show, she was visibly more relaxed and more confident.

When the last show was over and we all finally wound

down and made it to bed, I started reflecting on the experience. That's when the lightning bolt hit me. Just like I know my children—know their interests and talents—God knows me and what I'm best suited for. In the same way I had immediately recognized that the casting call had Lauren's name written all over it, my Father presents me with tailor-made opportunities to use the gifts he's given me.

"This is perfect for you!" he says. "This is your thing!"

However, I know that I often walk away.

The paper-thin excuses never end. Maybe the preparation is too hard, like those weeks of long practices. Maybe the process is too intimidating, like auditioning in front of all those strangers. Maybe the fear of failure and the unknown is stronger than the joy of obedience.

Often, I am so accustomed to hearing the inner critic that I don't recognize when it sneaks in dressed as reasoning thought. *What if?* it says, or *Let me think about it.* The worst is *Yes, but . . . ,* which is just another way of saying no.

That's when the opportunity slips away. God never forces me. But I miss the blessing and the chance to be a blessing when I tell God, "Not me, not now."

Oh, he'll get some other people blessed; I just won't get to be a part of it, and that's my loss.

One of my favorite parts of going to Lauren's shows, I have to admit, was hearing the compliments she received. (That whole childbirth process, I think, entitles me to share in the compliments.) Likewise, when I am obedient and throw myself into the opportunities God lays before me, he gets glory from it. Doing those things that bring honor and glory to God is what I was made for, and they are the only things I have to give back to my Father.

When Lauren joined the cast, she took on certain responsibilities, but there was far more that she didn't have to worry about. Building the sets, making the costumes, promoting the show, even setting the rehearsal schedule were all other people's jobs. Yet when she and everyone else in the cast and crew hit their mark, everything that had been coordinated around her came together as well. The results were a delight to everyone who saw the show.

I need to remember that with each opening God gives me, he has synchronized the rest of his cast and engineered the circumstances to produce his desired results. He even tells that to Isaiah the prophet: "It will all happen as I have planned. It will be as I have decided. . . . The LORD of Heaven's Armies has spoken—who can change his plans? When his hand is raised, who can stop him?" (Isaiah 14:24, 27).

What did Lauren take away from the show besides wonderful memories? She saw that she has something to contribute, that she can be a significant part of something bigger than herself. She wears confidence like a favorite T-shirt now. Before, she may have suspected, but now she knows she has the right stuff. She's been tested, so she won't hesitate at all when the next opportunity comes along.

What did I take away? A question: If God has guaranteed the results, why do I waver? And a prayer: "God, help me remember that if you give the opportunity, you will bring success. Please, don't stop giving me chances even when I'm afraid to take them."

—Paula Wiseman

TRASH ACCOUNTS

I was drained in body, soul, and spirit.

Christmas was over, and all the hustle and bustle of the holiday season had left me exhausted. As I struggled to open my eyes one morning, I had a choice. I could sit and veg out all day, or I could do something productive.

I decided to do the latter. As I glanced around my home, I knew some work and TLC was desperately needed. Holiday boxes, bags, cards, papers, and other things still cluttered the rooms. I felt a little overwhelmed by the task but gathered my courage and grabbed trash bags to begin decluttering.

Taking that first step is the hardest thing to do. But as I took that first step toward eliminating the clutter, it led to a day of total liberation. Out with the old and in with the new, right? The process was actually producing freedom and relief in my heart. And my timing was perfect—our neighborhood trash pickup was the next day.

As dawn arrived, I decided to drag all the trash out myself because my teenage boys were still sleeping. I carefully placed all the bags and boxes at the end of our driveway and was quite proud of myself for having them out on time.

I was also pleased that I had achieved my goal of eliminating the holiday clutter. I remember hearing the trash truck later that morning but didn't think much about it. After all, that was a regular midweek sound. I was so thrilled that all those bags and boxes would finally be off my property that I didn't worry a bit. The minimountain at the end of our driveway would be gone forever.

As I glanced out of my office window later that day, I was shocked to see the minimountain still in place, without even one box or bag moved!

What's up with that? I thought. All our neighbors' trash was gone—only ours was still there. Irritation started to wash over me. *Maybe the trash men just overlooked our side of the street. Maybe the glare off the snow impaired their vision for a few minutes right at the intersection of the street and our driveway. After all, they had to move quickly to get the entire neighborhood's holiday trash picked up.*

I continued to reason with myself—they could have been tired, as I was, in this postholiday season. After all, where is my compassion for those trashmen after the holidays? It was a chore to go out every day and pick up people's trash. I wouldn't want that job.

Realizing they weren't coming back to pick up my trash, I sent the boys to move it all back into our garage. The minimountain moved back, to take up residence once more until the next week.

By the time the next trash pickup date arrived, the minimountain had grown to a full-grown mountain with nothing mini about it! It had gone from lining one side of the garage to taking up half a parking space. We faced the challenge of trying to put the car back into its home in the garage. Imagine this holiday trash equation in your home: two weeks of normal trash + holiday trash + boxes = one big mountain of trash!

The boys woke up early to help me move all the trash back to the edge of the driveway. Let's just say we were now making a statement in the neighborhood—I'm not sure what that statement was, unless it was to say we have lots of trash at our house or we are trashy!

This time I was praying for the trashmen to come quickly. I opened the blinds so I could see the trash truck arrive and the trashmen clear it all away. At this point, all I wanted for the New Year was for this mountain to be moved.

I couldn't believe my eyes. It happened all over again. I saw the trash truck pull up and clear away all the neighbors' trash but ignore the mountain at the end of our driveway. Now I was definitely not a happy camper, nor did I qualify for a satisfied trash customer!

"Aren't there responsible trashmen on my route? How could they ignore seeing that large trash mountain right beside the road? This is ridiculous!"

It took quite a bit of time to haul it all back into the garage at this point, but we did. Believe me, not only were things looking bad in our garage, but the smell was getting putrid. I headed to the phone, muttering unkind things concerning our trash service.

Locating and dialing the trash-service number, I asked for customer service immediately. In my nice voice, I explained the scenario of having our trash ignored for the past two weeks. The representative asked for our current address and account number. The account number I had was not correct, so she pulled up my address. At that point, the customer service rep became strangely quiet.

"What is wrong?" I asked.

"Ma'am, I cannot locate an account for you."

"What? That doesn't make any sense. We've had our trash picked up here for three years. We've never faced an issue with it until two weeks ago."

"Ma'am, we have just completed a trash audit for all our customers. I'm not locating your name or address on our current customer list—I don't see an account having been created for your household. The last record we have for your address is for another name three years ago, and that service was discontinued the day he moved out. Our records show that no one has continued service at that address since then."

I couldn't believe what I was hearing! We were not on their list? How could that have happened? After all, our trash had been picked up midweek for the past three years with no problems. Our understanding was that the trash service was included in our other monthly utility bills, just like in our other home. We had paid all those bills on time and never had any issues surface until now.

So the realization sank in: We were not real trash customers at all! Obviously, the trashmen were not in error. We were. We had not ever set up a trash account for service.

My anger dissipated. I quickly set up an account so we would be taken care of in the future. The customer service representative promised it would be picked up the next week. Though the trash mountain had been irritating to deal with, I had just received news that we had been free from all trash-service fees for the past three years!

What an unexpected gift we had been given, and we didn't even know it! My whole perspective changed instantly when I realized the truth about our trash dilemma. Isn't that how it works out in life sometimes? The truth can truly set us free to have different attitudes and perspectives. A great lesson to remember is to slow down, wait to react, and make sure we discover the real truth about life's scenarios. As a result, we could learn to develop and possess a whole new attitude in living.

The next week I heard the trash truck approaching. Believe me, this was music to my ears. All our accumulated trash and holiday collection was at the end of our driveway—again. Let's just say it was a present waiting to be discovered by the trashmen. As I watched them load all those items into that trash truck, I applauded wildly. My decluttering project had turned into a growing, stinking, three-week-old, erupting trash volcano in my garage. Thankfully, it was finally gone! I was celebrating with freedom in my body, soul, and spirit that day.

Through this trash-account experience, I learned several lessons: One is the importance of operating and walking in truth and learning to watch and be thankful for those blessings that unexpectedly enter our lives. How could I forget the waiver of three years of trash fees? Instead of always reacting in life, I needed to learn to respond with a heart of gratitude in situations as I try to focus on the positive. I needed to learn to take time to let God speak to me and teach me through the everyday life situations that surround me.

Proverbs 15:14 tells us, "A wise person is hungry for knowledge, while the fool feeds on trash."

Do I have any trash in my life, Lord? Is anything accumulating in the garage of my heart?

Today was the day for decluttering my soul and spirit as I let his account be the ruling force in my life. John 8:32 says, "You will know the truth, and the truth will set you free."

The truth of Jesus Christ can set us free from living with trash in any area of our lives. He truly is the only one to set up an account with for the rest of eternity. And he is always timely.

—Jamie Speak Wooten

Remember the children's song about the wheels on the school bus going round and round? That precious childhood tune always brought back so many memories of being joyful and carefree—until my son, one day, showed me another meaning to this once-captivating song.

Justin, my middle child, holds more energy than he knows what to do with. He is all boy! Most days, my only hope is to be prepared for whatever antics he might display.

One such incident caught me completely off guard. My handsome, brown-eyed son came bounding through the front door after a full day of first grade. He found me lounging on the couch in my customary 3 P.M. position—feet up and TV on, watching the Food Network channel.

Needless to say, my stomach was ready and my soul longed to be with the hostess, tasting her masterpiece of perfection! But, as life would have it, the sound of my whimpering son quickly brought me back to reality.

"Mom, the school bus driver wants to see you—*now!*" he cried. I sat there bewildered, wondering what had just happened to my peaceful little world of pasta and cheese. I quickly looked at Justin and said, "What happened, buddy?"

He replied, "My school bus driver wants to see you *now*. She's parked outside the house!"

Outside the house? I thought. I asked, "Why?" as I jumped off the couch.

Apprehension filled me, and I knew I needed to brace myself. As I walked to the front door, I probed Justin for more information, but he would say only, "I don't know."

Of course, that was a sure sign this situation was bad! As we approached the "scene of the crime," he looked deathly pale. The twenty-five-foot walk from my front door to the mailbox has never seemed so long as it was that day!

Sure enough, the big yellow school bus marked "639" was awaiting us.

Many years had passed since I last jumped on a school bus, but as I felt the heat from the engine and heard the steady idle of the motor, I immediately felt seven years old again. The doors squealed open, and I saw those black, rubber-coated stairs. My heart pounded as I began to ascend them. On the third stair sat a blue-eyed, five-foot-two, gray-haired lady. Her hands covered her face, and she was sobbing. I swallowed hard and braced myself.

Finding the courage, I said, "Hi, Miss Donna. Justin said you wanted to see me?"

Her eyes filled with more tears and panic as they met mine. The poor lady was shaken, and my heart went out to her, but I also felt protective of my son. I swallowed hard as I could hear the guilty verdict spoken over Justin.

Miss Donna explained how Justin had entertained the other passengers by standing in his seat and throwing his body halfway outside the school bus window while screaming at the top of his lungs. Mind you, the bus was going fifty-five miles per hour down the local highway! She exclaimed how she heard chanting and clapping as Justin performed his death-defying act of folly.

Leave it to my son to lead an uprising to overcome boredom on a school bus! Looking into her mirror, Miss Donna had witnessed Justin's body balancing on the window frame. Frightened and alarmed, she knew that if she hit her brakes or jerked the bus in either direction, Justin would fall out and either get crushed by the bus wheels or get hit by another vehicle.

Somehow, she kept control of her emotions, slowed down the bus, and dealt with the situation. In her thirty years of service as a school bus driver, she had never experienced such a terrifying situation. Leave it to my son to challenge her world!

I stood speechless. I wished I could quickly read a parenting book directing me on "How to deal with out-of-control boys who love the center of attention on the school bus"!

Justin started crying behind me, and I felt trapped in the middle of having compassion for both him and Miss Donna. What should I do? My natural instinct was to take my son and spank him till the cows came home, but I knew that I would be doing it out of anger rather than love if I laid a hand on him at that moment.

Finally, I took a deep breath and hugged the bus driver, trying to comfort her. I told both of them that God had watched over them that afternoon. I apologized for my son's behavior and required Justin to apologize. Miss Donna told me she would have to report the incident to the principal. I told her I understood her position.

Justin and I walked back into our house. My son went to his room. Somehow, I quickly became calm. Usually, I would have ranted and screamed at the top of my lungs and added to the drama, but I felt God's presence. I just listened to his quiet voice inside me.

My Kingdom, my Kingdom, was all I could hear him say. It was about his Kingdom business. He replayed in my mind my hugging the driver; at first, she was hesitant, like nobody had ever comforted her before.

When I pointed out to her that God had watched over them, I remembered that she surprisingly agreed. I saw a peace fill her, and I remembered feeling tranquil right then because I knew God was using all of us together to reveal something important to us individually.

God showed me how I could trust his protection over my children. Justin was learning humility, obedience, and authority, while Miss Donna discovered love, compassion, and shelter.

When my husband got home that afternoon, I briefed him on the event. We agreed that the punishment should fit the crime. Justin had to write an apology to Miss Donna, asking for her forgiveness. He also spent the evening writing all ten of his bus rules, five times each. For a first grader, this was a lot of writing. I could hear him at the kitchen table muttering how he wished there were only five rules.

I chuckled because although he had committed a serious act, he is still just a kid—a kid looking for fun and adventure, living life with zeal and no boundaries. But through this punishment, he learned another important lesson: A person gifted with leadership must take his influence and use it appropriately to glorify God under the boundaries he sets for us. I praised God for the much-needed lesson—one we all need reminding of from time to time.

The next day at school, the principal summoned Justin to her office to meet with the bus driver. They graciously allowed him to continue riding the bus, but the principal restricted him to the front seat behind the driver. Justin was upset at first, but eventually he understood that consequences always follow actions—whether good or bad. Miss Donna and Justin eventually became good friends. She favors Justin now, and since then, she has told me how he makes her laugh.

Trusting the Lord throughout life is always difficult. But God has a funny way of taking the simple things in life—such as school buses and children—and using them to reveal keys to his Kingdom. We gain wisdom much quicker when we walk in these situations firsthand. Who knew that as "the wheels on the bus went round and round" that day, God was the driver? Scripture tells us that God has been faithful to a thousand generations (see Deuteronomy 7:9). In my book, that equates to thousands of school-bus miles!

—Kimchi Lya Blow

BECOMING THE PERFECT HOSTESS

I attended the perfect holiday party once. You know the kind—the one thrown by Mr. & Mrs. Perfect Hosts. The table was resplendent with gorgeous china and linens that matched. Centerpieces looked like museum works of art, and the crystal glasses were spotless. The subdued lighting created an intimate mood, and the tables were laden with food that looked too perfect to eat. What made me even more envious was the genuine hospitality displayed by the host and hostess—they made everyone feel right at home.

I felt like such a failure as I held myself up to their impeccable example. I had always envied people who entertained with such finesse. I was jealous of those who, unlike me, had stainless carpet, matching furniture, fine linens with no holes, crystal stemware with no nicks, fine china with no scratches, and polished sterling silverware.

I lacked the social graces necessary to evoke any appreciative "aahs" from people who entered my home. So I rarely entertained. Then one day my perception of what makes a perfect hostess dramatically changed.

Ten of us weary souls were covered in a thin, grimy film—our own sweat mixed with the fine, powdery dust of Tanzania. The women had been busy all day performing puppet shows for eight hundred children and distributing crafts and coloring sheets. The men had been building benches for the local church. It was dinnertime, and we trudged down the dusty road from our spartan accommodations at the guest lodge in the remote Maasai village of Mairowa in East Africa.

Our flashlights illuminated the rocky path before us. As we rounded the corner of the trail, we saw the tiny house where Isack and Asnath, indigenous missionaries to the village, lived. We crammed our dirty bodies into the miniscule living room. We were an exhausted group of *wuzungus* (white people), and we stared at two flickering candles on the coffee table as we waited for dinner.

The candles weren't there for atmosphere—the home had no electricity. The eight-by-ten-foot room was furnished with a coffee table, a twin bed, a sofa, a loveseat, and two wooden chairs. Above the bed was a screenless window, and a threadbare curtain fluttered in the breeze. The walls were papered with newsprint. We had to wedge sideways between the coffee table and the sofa to sit down. I plopped wearily onto the bed, which also served as a sofa, and curiously looked around the room to discover any hints of what might be for dinner. I couldn't decide whether I was more hungry or tired.

Our hostess, Asnath, shuffled into the room, smiling broadly, and spoke softly, "Welcome." She continued in halting English, "Thank you so much for coming. You are so welcome here."

Her hands held a carafe of something. We passed around some coffee cups, and Asnath asked if we wanted some milk.

That's good, I thought, *some cold skim milk to soothe my parched throat.*

I had been breathing the thick dust of the village all day. I could mentally taste the cold milk already. I waited eagerly as Asnath filled the cups. But when I had a full cup in my hand, I stared at a thick, creamy, steaming beverage. What was this? I sipped it. Not bad, but not exactly what my tongue and throat had anticipated. Back in the States, I drank only icy cold skim milk, so this was a vastly different taste sensation. It was thick and heavy, almost like cream. It was mildly sweet and flavorful. I wondered what it could be—goat's milk, perhaps?

We joined hands and prayed, in English and Maa, a prayer of thanksgiving for our safe arrival, for the tasks we had accomplished that day, and now for this meal. Our dinner consisted of a casserole of noodles and baked potatoes, raw carrots, and goat stew. As we juggled plates on our laps, I watched Asnath. She dished up our meals from a long, narrow wooden table in the corner of the room. She kept going outside to bring in more food.

I realized that she didn't have a kitchen. She'd prepared this meal while stooping over an open fire. She asked if we wanted second helpings. Some of the men asked for more, but I was too tired to chew! I noticed that Asnath never ate. I didn't know if she had already eaten or if she was waiting to make sure her American guests had plenty to eat.

I knew she must be tired; she walked all over the village of Mairowa to teach and train the women. She also had a young daughter to look after.

As we ate, a Maasai warrior entered and stood in the corner, his *shuka* (traditional blanket) draped over one shoulder. A chicken hopped across the threshold and joined us, scratching in the dirt scattered on the concrete floor. It kept darting under the table and bed as I surreptitiously tried to shoo it away from my feet. The chicken finally jumped on the bed and escaped through the window.

Asnath seemed oblivious to the chicken's antics; she showed no embarrassment that a chicken was in her living room. I would have been mortified if some barnyard animal had entered my house while I was entertaining! Asnath dished up a hearty plate for the warrior. He ate silently and left, barely glancing at the disheveled guests. Asnath smiled as she continued to meet our needs and fill our stomachs.

After we finished eating, she gathered the dirty dishes and took them outside, presumably to wash them in a plastic bucket, though water was a scarce and valuable commodity here. Outside her house was a concrete cistern filled with sand that filtered the rainwater. She and her husband had built it themselves.

I marveled at Asnath's hospitality. She did not have what I considered to be the basic essentials to entertain—indoor plumbing to start with, not to mention a refrigerator, stove, or microwave. We're not even talking about the accoutrements of fine table linens or matching plates and polished silverware. She did not have a quality dining table with matching chairs, a lovely lighted buffet filled with matching serving pieces, or an elegant centerpiece. Yet I had never experienced such hospitality.

I was suddenly ashamed as I thought of my spacious apartment where I never entertained guests. I had justified myself by saying I didn't have enough space to entertain or didn't have the time to clean the house. I realized that true hospitality was not about surroundings but about a heart attitude. I saw true hospitality in Africa in this tiny concrete home, where food was lovingly prepared and served with a servant's heart.

Asnath gave what she had, willingly and without excuses, to those God had brought all the way from America to her tiny abode. How much more generous I should be with all God has given me, yet I have hoarded it and made feeble excuses. I promised myself that when I got back home, I would entertain more and worry less about having the perfect table setting or perfectly clean house. It wasn't my house after all, but God's. I was reminded of Romans 12:13: "When God's people are in need, be ready to help them. Always be eager to practice hospitality."

As we left, I viewed our surroundings with different eyes. I hugged thin Asnath, whispering "Mungu akubariki" ("God bless you") in her ear. My brief words of thanks were not just for her hospitality, but also for the powerful and wordless lesson she had taught me that transcended language barriers: True hospitality begins with a servant's heart, not an elaborate set of fine china and stemware.

Oh, in case you're wondering what the mystery beverage was—I was wrong, it wasn't goat's milk after all. It was camel's milk.

—Connie Dunn

WHEN HORMONES
SPOIL THE FRUIT

There they come again: the sudden heat that makes my body feel as if it's on fire, the night sweats that leave me swimming in my sheets, the mood swings that make me go from "zero to witch" in sixty seconds or less.

I used to have a mind. I used to have a memory. Those days seem a distant dream as I find myself hormonally challenged. How about you?

You may be hormonally challenged if

your children are confused about their correct names because you get them mixed up so often;

you look in the mirror and say, "Help! My face has fallen, and it won't get up!"

you wonder where your memory went (among other things) and find yourself praying often for it to return.

My doctor tried me on low-dose hormone therapy. After a few months, I noticed hair cascading to my shoulders. I wasn't too alarmed until I realized that was because it was falling out. When I tried hair regrowth formula, I did notice new hair growing. But I was trying for hair on my head, not facial or nose hair.

Sometimes I feel like I am ready to climb the walls. One moment I will feel fine, and the next moment I would like to flee this body that has become a stranger to me. I feel like my friends and family can't possibly know the "real me" because I don't even recognize me at times.

Is this what the normal perimenopausal woman goes through? I wondered. If this roller-coaster ride is "normal," please stop and let me off!

I admit hormones are a challenge, even for people of faith. It is hard to display the fruits of the Spirit—love, joy, peace . . . and especially self-control (see Galatians 5:22-23)— when your hormones are raging. I have a new compassion for Martha, who in Luke 10:40 confronted Jesus about all she had to do and how little her sister, Mary, was helping. We get the idea Martha was this busy sister, when perhaps she was actually trying to get relief from her hormones. Have you ever felt that way yourself?

I asked one of my daughters what things I did that seemed to indicate I was hormonally challenged. She said she noticed that sometimes I rant and rave and then pick up a ringing phone as a completely different person—a nicer, quieter person.

So, let me see, is she saying I yell? No, that can't be. I have a Southern drawl and am gentle and smiling.

"Yelling? You say I yell? My mother yelled, but not me!" I told her.

Then my daughter said, "What about when the telephone solicitors call or the pizza order is wrong?"

Was she saying I don't have the right to complain about pizza orders? Does this sound like I am acting out my hormones? "Hello, is this Pizza Perfect, where the customer is always happy? I'm not happy! I ordered three orders of mushrooms not just three mushrooms. Just because I order fast food doesn't mean my kids don't eat vegetables. Haven't you heard about the four basic food groups? My kids need their mushrooms for a balanced diet. Make me happy or the thirty dollars a week I spend with you will go elsewhere."

And telephone solicitors always seem to call either when I'm cooking, vacuuming, homeschooling, or gathering everybody to the table for a family supper. It's hard not to act hormonal as I try to explain politely why I never buy anything over the telephone, and they just keep talking. I've been tempted to ask for their phone number so I can call *them* during supper. But I wouldn't do that . . . or maybe these days I would! Blame it on the hormones!

When seeing something the children did wrong turns me ballistic, am I having a hormonal moment? Is it PMS, or have we gone way past even that excuse? Now there is a new disorder named PMDD (premenstrual dysphoric disorder), which goes beyond physical symptoms and deals with the more-emotional side effects.

We were watching television one night when a commercial listed symptoms that screamed my name. As I was sitting there, face burning, knowing my family was going to say, "That's what you act like!" my seventeen-year-old said timidly, "Could you have that?"

At such a moment, you are aware anew of the grace God gives through your family—they aren't there to condemn you; they really want you to feel better.

Usually the world isn't so caring. In fact, so far the nicest definition I've come up with for *PMS* is "Pretty Miserable Sister."

I'd heard so many women expound on the wonders of progesterone cream that I thought I'd try some. I checked the ingredients and saw that they were all natural, made with wild yams. But my eyes seemed to eliminate the word *estrogen* on the label, and I didn't contact my doctor before trying it. After I used the cream, my period started a week late and then continued for twelve long days. Believe me, I won't use that stuff again!

Sometimes a woman must weigh the risks from the drugs or hormones the doctor gives her and balance them against the challenge of living with hormonal changes. When I was at the height of my symptoms, I tried many alternatives and finally went back to a low-dose birth-control pill, at my doctor's suggestion. But my blood pressure went abnormally high, and I chose to go off the medicine. As a result, I felt like biting somebody at times.

Men also have to bear the challenge of hormones. We have all heard of men in "midlife crisis," where in a moment of insanity they leave wonderful families to run away with a Barbie girl. Or as my brother-in-law says, "I know all about hormones and what to do. When she's hot, I put on a sweater because I know the air-conditioning is going to be set on freezing."

Now that I have this disorder, I recognize it everywhere. When my children come home from school complaining about the frigid temperature in their classroom (they swear icicles hang from their bodies), I just bundle them up in coats as I send them out into ninety-degree weather. I realize their poor schoolteacher has not only schoolchildren to contend with, but also hot flashes!

Some of the best relief from the challenge of changing hormones is the comfort of discovering other women are going through the same thing. Knowing that I am not the only one going through night sweats, hot flashes, and witchy behavior helps me through the day. Just knowing someone is praying that I can control my emotions sometimes gives me the ability I need to do just that.

I may not always exhibit all the fruits of the Spirit, but I take solace in the thought that the God who created hormones understands hormonal women. And thankfully, grace is what he's all about—even on the days when hormones seem to spoil the fruit. In fact, for most of us, at this and any stage of life, we can relate to Paul when he says in Romans, "I don't really understand myself, for I want to do what is right, but I don't do it. Instead, I do what I hate. . . . I want to do what is right, but I can't. I want to do what is good, but I don't. I don't want to do what is wrong, but I do it anyway. . . . I love God's law with all my heart. But there is another power within me that is at war with my mind." (7:15, 18-19, 22-23)

In my weak, hormonal nature, God's power is still strong.

My friends and I can laugh together and cry together and pray together over our hormonal happenings. And when the children bring me a broom, I know they are being helpful and thinking I want to clean house—not thinking I misplaced my mode of transportation.

—Donna Collins Tinsley

THE HAIRY SPIDER
WITH NINE LIVES

The ugly, hairy spider and I had a face-off in the walk-in pantry.

I had not invited him in, and I was determined to do everything I had learned in my two decades of critter combat to make him go away. I wanted him to rue the day he ever set feet—all eight of them—on the same shelf as my peanut butter and pickle jars.

Fearlessly, I scanned the pantry for a weapon. Or two. One can never be overly equipped, you know, when it comes to arachnid warfare.

I looked down and spotted the perfect whacking device. My left shoe. (I knew I would need the other one to rush me to safety in case of a retaliatory counterattack on the part of my ferocious foe.)

Off with the shoe. On with the battle. We flew into action, my shoe and I.

Whop! WHOP! WHOP! I was relentless.

Bam! BAM! BAM! He was invincible.

With every blow, he bounced back up. The harder I'd pound, the higher he'd jump. Time for rearmament . . . call for reinforcements!

I grabbed the *Stars and Stripes* newspaper out of the trash, quickly transformed it into a billy club, and modified my plan. I would strategically anticipate which direction he would jump after the shoe hit him, and I would smack him on the fly, so to speak, with the *Stars and Stripes*. It seemed almost unpatriotic, but I was desperate.

The plan was a flop; my leaping opponent remained victorious. But I was not giving up. I was determined to continue my rolled-up-newspaper-to-the-jugular defense to the bitter end, when I heard my husband yelling from the living room.

"What's going on in there, World War III?"

"He won't die!" I screamed back.

My gallant knight-in-shining-armor burst into the pantry where the two of us, human versus beast, had been duking it out. Actually, I was the only one duking, I suppose, but the spider was not cooperating. It appeared that my lethal weapons were somehow no match for his incredible fortitude.

"Step aside," my brave new spouse commanded.

"My hero," I cooed.

Impressed with his bravery, awed by his courage, I watched him reach down, bare-handed, to pick up the spider, who by now had leaped off the shelf onto the floor. I turned away and covered my eyes.

"Look," he said.

"I can't!" I countered.

"Look, Sandi," he insisted.

"O-o-o-h, no, I can't look!"

Finally, I looked. There, in the palm of his hand, was a large, wadded-up rubber band, covered with hair from my ponytail, which I had taken out earlier that morning.

The hairy spider with nine lives.

If rubber bands could talk, I'm sure this one would've had a story that even his own mother would never believe: "There I was, minding my own business, Mama, honest, when this wild woman, armed to the teeth, came at me and kept thwacking and . . ." Well, maybe rubber bands can't talk, but they sure can jump.

Believe it or not, I've discovered a valuable lesson in this encounter. It's about bouncing back from the blows of adversity. In Romans 5:3-4 the apostle Paul tells us, "We can rejoice, too, when we run into problems and trials, for we know that they help us develop endurance. And endurance develops strength of character, and character strengthens our confident hope of salvation."

Imagine being that rubber band, enduring such trauma. Perhaps you've been there—perched on the shelf of innocence, clobbered by blows of injustice:

> You've been pounded and battered in ways that seem unfair, misguided, or downright wrong.
> You've suffered at the hand of a relative or from the tongue of a friend.
> You trusted people. They betrayed you.
> You shared a secret. They spread the word.
> You finally opened the door to your heart. He crushed it.
> You raised your child in the faith. She turned away from it.
> You took good care of your body. It's laid you up or let you down.

Beloved, I wish it were not so. I think of my own loved ones who suffer courageously in the midst of illness and heartache;

I watch and wait and weep, and I secretly wish that the word *suffering* could be stricken from every area of life—physical, emotional, relational, financial, spiritual, mental.

I wish life could be without wrongs or that all wrongs would be righted. I wish we could push the "undo/redo" arrow on the keyboard of life choices or start over with a fresh document and rewrite parts of our life's screenplay with a new script, new dialogue, maybe even new players.

I wish we could erase the scoreboard and be allowed to keep hitting until we knock one out of the ballpark to the cheer of the crowd and the thrill of a parent. I wish all the feelings of failure, all the aftermath of brokenness, all the giants of fear were never allowed on the playing field.

And I wish we could remove all the *S* pages from the dictionary, where *sadness* and *sin* and *sorrow* and *suffering* reside.

Or do I? As soon as I'm certain the answer is "Yes!" to all the above, I read a passage like Romans 5:3-4 again: "We can rejoice, too, when we run into problems and trials, for we know that they help us develop endurance. And endurance develops strength of character, and character strengthens our confident hope of salvation." And then I remember that the apostle Paul, who wrote these words, also wrote his greatest treatise on joy and encouragement, not while lounging comfortably in a La-Z-Boy recliner but while suffering in prison.

I discover that he uses the word *suffering* as one might use the word *blessing.* And I realize that if we removed all the *S* pages from the dictionary, we would miss the wonders of *Savior, sufficient, satisfied, streams, spirit,* and *singing.* We would not taste the sweetness of God's Word, or hear the sound of his still, small voice. We would not know the sovereignty and shepherding and saving grace that are his, or the salvation and strength and spiritual gifts that can be ours when we put our faith in him.

If we removed all the negatives of life, we would never know all the riches of God's glory or his best gifts for his children, because they come beautifully wrapped together in a package: heartache and joy, pain and perseverance, rain and sunshine, undergoing and overcoming, trials and trust.

Isn't it intriguing that the words *good, right,* and *fair* coexist happily in the dictionary with the words *bad, wrong,* and *unfair?* And that *problems* and *trials* live peacefully beside *rejoice* and *hope* in the same Scripture verse?

I don't know about you, but when I'm sitting quietly on the shelf of life and am suddenly attacked by harsh blows, it's comforting to know that they're not the work of some weapon-wielding, wild woman. Instead, the Bible assures us they are allowed by our loving and sovereign God, precisely measured to produce endurance and character and perfectly planned to work for our good and his glory.

As Charles Stanley, a Southern Baptist preacher, explains, "God wants us to have an unshakable faith—and if trials, tests, and suffering are what it takes for us to have it, then he'll allow them."

We are all destined to suffer and sigh. But God provides the resources to enable us to bounce back from adversity:

His Word shows us what to do.
His Spirit empowers us to do it.
His Son has made it all possible by his sacrifice
   at Calvary.

And if we look carefully, we will find that often in our deepest sorrows and our darkest valleys, his comforting presence, his amazing grace, and his wondrous love seem to shine the brightest.

That should make us want to leap . . . for joy!

—Sandi Banks

MY SISTER'S NEIGHBOR

I held the door open while my husband and brother-in-law squeezed as many boxes as they could onto the elevator floor. The odor of wet carpet mingled with curry hung in the air of the dim hallway. A serenade of muffled sitcoms, the creaking of stairwell doors, the thumping of garbage disposals, and the occasional wail of a child was a familiar melody I had long forgotten.

The apartment building looked like any other, but behind door number 523 was a quaint little bachelor suite, no larger than my bedroom at home. The kitchen—eight tiles large—had room for one person to stand and scrape pots, with a view to the living room by day and the bedroom by night. The cupboard had ample room for two cans of soup and one box of croutons—if that box of croutons served four.

During our travels to and from the elevator, we passed several unfamiliar faces. Each person we encountered that night either had a bad case of shifty eyes, was running from a boyfriend, or was mumbling what sounded like, "They all must die."

"Oh, I just remembered," my sister, Gloria, said, opening her door, "the landlord warned me that there are some people in the building I may want to stay away from and that I should probably keep to myself."

Normally, when someone warns me to keep to myself, I don't go visiting strangers in their apartments. However, curiosity often makes it difficult to stick with that plan.

My foray started very innocently: An elderly lady barely taller than a toy poodle poked her head of curlers into the hallway before placing her slippered foot outside her home. Standing in the doorway, she watched us drag lamps and pillows from the elevator, then pulled a tattered tissue from the sleeve of her turquoise dress. Wiping her nose, the elderly woman looked my way and whispered, "Come here," motioning with a small, crooked finger. I was torn between curiosity and caution, but caution leaped out the window and curiosity sprinted toward the old woman's door.

Ps-s-s-t, she whispered. Her red lips were thin and wrinkled like Twizzlers. "Are you moving in?"

"No," I explained, "my sister is moving in."

Like a newborn baby rooting around for milk, she glanced up and down the halls before echoing the words of their landlord, "Tell her to keep to herself; there are some strange people in this building."

Curiosity raced at full speed, like a pregnant woman trying to hail a Baskin-Robbins truck. I had to find out what was going on, so I asked, "What do you mean?"

When she pulled me close to whisper in my ear, I realized I had just crossed the border from Acquaintance Town to Best-Friends-ville. "Tell her to watch out," she said, pointing down the hall. "That guy over there is a rapist."

"A therapist?" I asked, stunned by the words that might have just escaped her lips.

Holding her mouth so close to my face that I could smell her Tetley tea, she snapped, "A rapist!"

The uneasy feeling told me that it was time to leave. She, on the other hand, decided it was time I came in to visit. She grabbed my arm, beckoning me to tour her shoe-box apartment. Since the day the home and garden television shows started airing "My Home Is Nicer than Yours" and "My Carpenter Is Hotter than Yours," no woman has refused the proposal of a tour. Instinct told me to run—and run fast—but I didn't want to be the first woman to break with tradition. So I stepped through her door.

To my surprise, the apartment was à la Martha, after her prison term. It was a quaint little home, shadowed by flickering candles that lit up antiques and emitted the smells of dewberry and cinnamon into the air. An overabundance of fabric was draped through the rods surrounding her bed, dividing the Sealy Posturepedic with its calico quilts from the parlor.

Awaiting the arrival of Charles and Camilla, the coffee table was set with Royal Albert teacups and shiny teaspoons. Chocolates and cookies decorated the plates, and I wondered how long she had waited for someone to share them with her. Antique photos in ornate frames sat on the Duncan Phyfe tables, while tapestry pillows lined the back of the couch. The finest drapery fabrics were hugging each window, my new best friend was hugging my waist, and her silver head crowned with pink curlers was stabbing my chest.

Looking down at the little woman clinging tightly to me, I got the feeling that this lady's cookie jar was filled to the brim with crackers. The landlord's words echoed in my brain like a talking doll whose batteries were so low it sounded like

Chucky. The warning of his words burning in my ears told me it was definitely time to pull and run!

In an attempt to entice me to stay, she pointed to the photo of her charming grandfather on the table by the door. "There's the old Nazi," she said. As much as I was enjoying this little cuddle with the Nazi's granddaughter, I knew there were sane people on the other side of the door that I needed to get to.

My husband liberated me with a knock on the door. "Darlene, it's time for us to go," he said.

As I reached for the handle, she pointed her finger to my nose, "Tell your sister to stay away from Fatso in that other apartment I showed you!"

I left her apartment so fast I nearly fell into my sister's apartment. I slammed the door on the old lady who was hot on our heels.

In the comfort of my bed that night, I reflected on the evening and the woman I had met.

What will old age bring my way? I wondered. *Will I live alone? Will my family come to visit? Will I be able to fit a box of Preparation H in that cupboard? Will the cheese slip off my cracker?*

The next day, I shared the story with my mother, who echoed my conscience, asking, "What would Jesus have done?"

I knew it was a good question—one I should have considered before I fled her apartment, before I slammed the door, and before I covered the peephole with my finger, but sometimes it takes a wiser person to remind us to listen to the Spirit.

I think that Jesus would have stayed to have tea. He

would have tasted her cookies while he reclined on her couch. He would have listened to her stories of Grandpa, the Nazi. And he would have hugged her much more than she hugged him. I should have loved this person like he would have.

Yet all the while, I feared this woman who, like so many others that I have met in the past, differed from me. And likewise, there are, no doubt, some people who also fear me for the same reason. When I think about our differences, I am thankful for the trials I have faced and the influence the Spirit has had on shaping my soul. I have learned that the things that have made us different are the things that also make us the same.

Two people who face the same trials can share each other's pain, whereas another two can share sorrows that otherwise would not be understood. But it's important that we are letting the Spirit shape our soul—that we're listening to the voice that asks what Jesus would do, or what God would have us do, and that we're yielding to that voice.

We're all a little out of sorts from time to time. As I celebrate that uniqueness in all of us, I remember that Jesus loves each of us—including the scary ones—more than we know.

—Darlene Schacht

THE CHRISTMAS GIFT

Just a few days until Christmas . . . oh, how I loved this joyous season! My husband, Ted, and I continued the tradition we'd begun our first Christmas together—the previous year—when we'd been low on money but overflowing with love. We placed simple, handmade decorations on our Christmas tree.

As I prepared to celebrate Jesus' birth, my thoughts cartwheeled ahead to the anticipated birth of our first child. Perhaps my musings were similar to Mary's that first Christmas centuries ago. I wondered, *Will it be a boy or a girl? Am I really ready to be a mom?*

I had suffered a miscarriage the previous January and had experienced some problems with this pregnancy, so I felt anxious for a healthy delivery. Thankfully, holiday activities kept me from dwelling too much on the little one I longed to hold in my arms. Although at eight months' pregnant I felt like an overinflated balloon, I bustled about the house to get everything ready for Christmas and our baby.

The morning of December 23, I baked sugar cookies shaped like stars and bells and trees. Leaving dirty mixing bowls and cookie sheets on the kitchen counters, I hurried to my appointment at the obstetrician's office. Dr. Kim examined me and announced that my water was leaking. "I want you to check into the hospital by 5:00 P.M.," he said. "We're going to induce labor. And don't eat anything."

"Can't I wait till after Christmas?" I asked.

"No, there is danger of infection developing. The baby is big enough to survive."

Stunned, I returned home, called Ted at work, and then phoned our parents to tell them their first grandchild was about to be born. While I packed a bag, I felt more like I was acting in a play rather than experiencing reality.

This isn't how it is supposed to happen, I thought, fighting back tears. I peeked into the bedroom of our soon-to-be baby. Baby-shower gifts and sewing projects were piled around the unmade crib. I wanted to fix up this room and decorate it for our firstborn. *I guess I shouldn't have put it off.*

Ted drove me to the hospital. The maternity-ward nurse attached an IV to my arm and gave me Pitocin to stimulate contractions. With a fetal monitor strapped to my bulging abdomen, I had to lie on my back, which made the contractions intense.

My baby seemed to struggle to remain within its protective womb. I endured nineteen hours of labor and was not allowed to get up, eat, or even take a sip of water.

"Can't you let me go home for a while?" I begged. *If the baby wasn't ready, why should we force her to come early?* I wondered. Dr. Kim only smiled. Ted and my mother encouraged me, but I was hardly aware of their presence or that Christmas Eve day had dawned.

Finally, the nurse whisked me into the delivery room—my baby's heart rate had dropped. Instructing me to push, Dr. Kim grabbed the forceps and pulled out our premature daughter, who weighed less than six pounds.

He handed the baby to a pediatrician, Dr. Lee, who worked to get our little girl to breathe. I didn't even get a good look at our tiny daughter. Was she OK? How I wanted to hold her!

Dr. Lee placed the baby, her tiny body hooked to numerous wires and tubes, in an incubator in the nursery. Back in my room, I felt bereft. Ted and Mom had gone home to sleep after sitting with me all through labor. Not allowed to hold my baby or to have her near, I certainly didn't feel like a mother. Tears of sadness overflowed, rather than the tears of joy I had expected.

That lonely Christmas Eve, Dr. Lee solemnly told me, "Your daughter is not breathing well. I don't know if she will make it through the night. The next twelve hours are critical."

I felt crushed. I had yearned for our baby's birth, but now that Kathryn Elizabeth had arrived, I might lose her before I even got to touch her. Thoughts of Christmas and celebrations fled from my mind. *My baby might die before I get to cuddle her and tell her how much I love her.*

Tears kept me company that night. The joy of the season had totally disappeared. I prayed, entreating God to let me keep my precious Christmas gift. "Dear God, only you can make her live," I cried. "But, God, if she won't grow up to serve you, then please take her now to be with you. You know what is best." My words were as sincere as Mary's when she told the angel Gabriel, "May everything you have said about me come true" (Luke 1:38).

With those final words wrung from my heart, I tried to rest, awaiting Christmas morning.

Once again, Christmas morning brought good news

about a special birth. Dr. Lee looked relieved as he strode into my room. The crisis had passed. "It looks like your baby girl will live."

In fact, Kathy surprised the nursery staff with her increasing strength. When her tiny hand grasped the feeding tube and jerked it from her stomach, Dr. Lee decided not to replace it. She began taking nourishment by mouth.

After four days, I finally held our newborn daughter and felt like a real mom. When Kathy was six days old, we brought her home from the hospital. She began to thrive. The worst Christmas of my life had become my best Christmas ever. Now each year we have two wonderful births to celebrate!

—Mary A. Hake

TAKE A SEAT AT THE COUNTER

I wandered into a home-style chain restaurant one stifling morning. All my family members were out of town for the weekend, and I wanted a treat of home-cooked food without cooking for myself. My afternoon was free, my time was my own, and I had no demands or expectations from other people for the rest of the day. I was hungry and looking forward to a leisurely lunch in air-conditioned comfort.

Apparently I wasn't the only person with this thought, because the restaurant lobby was filled with families and other groups waiting for seating. I picked my way through the sea of people, approached the hostess's stand, and asked how long the wait would be.

"For how many?"

"Oh, just one," I replied casually.

I sat down on an available bench with a book to wait. I had developed the habit many years earlier of carrying a book with me at all times because I'm a voracious reader. I also discovered that having a book helps me wait more patiently. Delays become a guilty pleasure instead of an annoyance, and I escape from whatever crisis the world around me is experiencing.

I hadn't been reading very long when my name was called. The hostess asked if I'd mind sitting at the café-style counter near the kitchen. I hesitated. I am far from shy and quite capable of striking up a conversation with any random stranger, but I recharge my energy batteries by sinking into myself and having time with no conversation.

On this day, I wanted to read and be alone with my thoughts. My plans didn't call for any extra conversation or human interaction. I didn't want to sit at the counter because counters are not good places for introverts—it's difficult to maintain personal space and conversational walls while sitting on a stool at a counter. When strangers have to share elbow space while conveying fork to mouth, getting lost in a book is nearly impossible.

At the same time, insisting on a table just for one person would deprive another group of their seats and increase their waiting time, so I said, "That's fine."

I sat on a stool at the counter and opened my book. People get their meals faster when they sit at a counter, but something else happened that I didn't expect: I didn't want to focus on my book anymore. I kept it open, but I didn't care about the words on the page. I listened to people, instead. I heard what I thought was long gone: small-town, personalized service in a large metropolitan chain restaurant.

While I sat at that counter, several people came in and occupied stools near me. These people were apparently regulars because they were greeted by name, talked to, mock scolded, and made much of by all the servers as they assembled trays, refilled condiment bottles, and ferried orders around to tables.

An older gentleman with a speech impediment sat near me, and I instantly felt tongue-tied and shy. I was afraid he might speak to me, yet I was also afraid that failing to speak to him might somehow hurt him. As is so often the case in life, I found out this situation wasn't about me. This gentleman was the center of attention for several minutes as various staff members caught up on the circumstances of his life. They didn't even show a hint of impatience as each listened to this man.

One manager said she hadn't seen him come in for a meal for a while, and the gentleman mentioned having visited a rival restaurant. The manager scolded him, then chatted for a few more minutes before leaving. As she walked away, she reminded him, "Now remember: no more going to other restaurants!"

I marveled at the community I found when I wasn't looking for one. I went out for lunch and ended up getting more than food: I got an attitude adjustment I didn't even know I needed. I was afraid of the counter, afraid of community. I wanted to be solitary and self-centered. I didn't want the messiness of other lives bumping up against mine. I didn't want to modify my behavior to interact with others. I wanted to believe that I was self-sufficient. Despite my wishes, I ended up getting involved and was better for it.

Eating lunch at the counter reminded me that I can't inhabit this planet in seclusion or live my life alone. What I sometimes think will make my life easier actually makes it unbearable. I try to remove hassles and headaches and end up cutting out many wonderful things: community, conversation—and food!

Forget trying to remove the messiness of life. Life requires some friction, and that friction is what sharpens us. Choose to interact; choose to care. Step out of your comfort zone in some way and live, running into the tangles and confrontations of relationship. Take a seat at the counter.

—Susan Stanley

MAKING LITTLE THINGS BIG
AND BIG THINGS LITTLE

One of the heaviest things to carry is a box of books—I would never step on a scale while holding a box of books! Years ago when I was homeschooling, books piled up everywhere and sometimes threatened to take over. Not only did homeschooling make books and papers multiply on their own, but our whole family were avid readers, and we loved books!

After a while, though, the books seemed omnipresent, and I would put them in colorful plastic milk crates. We have a nice barn with a loft, and that was the storage place for our books. We left them there until I gave them away or sold them at a book sale.

We also have lots of cats in our barn—all over our land, for that matter. We live out in the middle of huge Wyoming wheat fields, where cats are necessary to take care of the mice that migrate in from the fields. Because we have hoards of field mice running all over the place, our cats are very important to us. My daughters always felt they were the most privileged kids in the world because they had kittens to spare.

On one of my "clean the books out of the house" days, I was carrying a box of books out to the barn. Just as I stepped off the porch, one of our tiniest kittens ran out from its hiding place and under my foot. It was a heart-stopping moment for me, and I was heartbroken when I saw the damage to the little yellow ball of fur. I knew death was inevitable for the baby kitten but was just sick to think it would not come quickly.

Of course, horrible events like this never go unwitnessed, and one of my young girls saw the whole thing. So besides my cries of dismay and the pitiful little mews of the kitten, the air was filled with my daughter's wailing. Soon all three of the girls had the mortally wounded kitten in a comfy, towel-lined box.

One of the girls looked up at me and said, "Mom, we need to pray. God can do anything, and he can fix this kitten as good as new."

I was really in a dilemma because even though I knew God could "fix" this terribly wounded kitten, I just didn't really believe he would. This seemed such an insignificant thing in God's economy of world and cosmic events—even though it held enormous consequences for the faith of three young girls.

I didn't feel much more positive when I prayed about a problem we were going through. We were facing a huge financial crisis with the IRS that had gone on for years, and it was beginning to look like we were going to lose everything we owned. Yes, I said I believed God could answer *all* our prayers, but I wasn't really sure he always did.

"Come on, Mom, let's pray!" the girls begged. Three pairs of expectant eyes looked at me, while the kitten cried agonizingly in the background. I was so afraid I would poke holes in their innocent faith, but I couldn't tell them, "No, don't bother God with this."

So we prayed, with each one taking turns asking God

for a miracle of healing. Their unwavering faith that God did care about their kitten took my breath away and scared me at the same time. I must admit my own prayer left God a lot of loopholes to work with. As the day progressed, not only did the kitten continue to live, but his unnatural bends began to straighten, and he quieted and slept.

Despite my faithless prayer, we did see God miraculously put this little kitten back together. Later, as a grown cat, he had the weirdest sounding *meow* I ever heard, but he did live.

On the other hand, the huge struggle with the IRS continued on like a big train coming down the tracks toward us. I felt as if we were helplessly tied to those tracks, watching inevitable disaster approach. Each morning I woke up with a feeling of dread. If God was not taking care of our *big* financial problem, why would he bother with a wounded kitten? Or is he just a God of little things, and we would have to hope for the best with the big things in our lives?

Then one day as I was making our bed, staring out the window and thinking of all we were going to lose, it hit me. The things that mattered in our lives were not even in the equation: Our marriage was good. My husband is a wonderful man and an even better father. No one was threatening to take the kids away. Everything that was really important would fit in the space of our bed! The rest was all just stuff! And you can always get more stuff.

Just as God used the faith of my little girls to pray that kitten back into wellness, God used our crisis to put my life into perspective. He taught me to live at peace in the midst of the storm. He didn't calm the storm around me right away, but he did calm the storm within me.

I have learned from those two experiences that with God little things are big and big things are little. He did eventually resolve our financial issues but not until the exact right moment. My daughters learned a big lesson in answered prayer, and I later learned to see what things are really big and what things really aren't.

—Karen Mackey

HELIUM PROMISES

"Now promise you won't cry when I leave." Adam's eyes sought mine.

"I promise," I mumbled and lowered my head. My words sounded good, but living them would be a daunting challenge.

"Are you sure, Mom?" Adam hooked a finger under my chin and raised it to look into my eyes once more. "I want to see your sweet smile when I drive off."

I nodded and pasted on my best fake smile. *Please, Lord, let me be brave. I'm about to come unglued.*

My eldest son was leaving home, heading to college. I'd known for years that this day would come and was certain I was ready for it.

I was not.

We were standing outside the bank when he made his no-tears admonition. He'd withdrawn some cash, tucked the traveling money in his wallet, and now jingled his car keys in his pocket. He was ready for this day.

Adam had spent the morning sorting and packing, deciding what to take and what childhood treasures to pack in attic-bound boxes and what to bury in the back of his closet. When I wasn't baking yet another batch of cookies to send with him, I leaned in his doorway and watched the process.

He seemed almost irreverent in the way he tossed around stuffed animals and young-reader books. He worked in rhythm with his radio, but by noon the radio was packed and the entry hall lined with a good share of his earthly possessions. He artfully crammed it all in his station wagon and lashed his bike to the roof rack. And though he couldn't see it, I slipped a chunk of my heart in that car too.

Just before he'd wormed his way into the driver's seat, Adam returned to the hallway and flipped to a handstand. The next chapter of his life lay before him, and I suspect the acrobatics were a celebration of this step toward independence.

For me, however, the handstand symbolized my "baby" leaving me. Hungry for every word and moment of that day, I captured him on film, upside down, knowing that in time I'd view the photograph with a misty smile.

"Earth to Mom . . ." Adam drew me back to the parking lot.

I hugged him for at least the twentieth time that day.

"Drive carefully," I said. "Do you have enough money for gas? Do you have everything you'll need right away? Call me when you get there. Good-bye! I love you!" The usual Mom litany. Surely my voice echoed mothers all across America in those last weeks of summer.

With patient indulgence, my almost-a-man son interpreted my questions. "Yup, Mom, I'll miss you, too." He gave me a final hug, said "I love you," squeezed back into his car, and drove off into his future.

I smiled bravely and waved for the few minutes it took his car to become a small dot in traffic. Then my smile faded.

I felt so alone, abandoned. The tears welling in my eyes turned to sobs, and I set aside my usual what-if-someone-sees-me attitude. It didn't matter who witnessed my misery. Anyway, I had no off switch for those tears. I dragged myself to my car and slouched behind the steering wheel.

"It's just not fair, God!" I blubbered and grabbed some tissues. Well, it wasn't fair. God sends our children to us as tiny, precious babies. We give all we've got to raising them, nurturing them, seeing them through illnesses and problems, laughing and crying with them, and next thing you know, they leave. Fresh tears fell. "Please help me, Lord. I'm just not doing well with this."

After a while, I pulled myself together and drove to the grocery store. Adam might be gone, but the rest of the family would expect dinner. My life seemed surreal, as if I existed on two levels. A major chapter of motherhood was ending—one of my offspring would no longer maintain his daily existence under the family roof. Yet other parts of my life would continue as usual. *Did anyone else struggle with this dichotomy?*

I grabbed a grocery cart and in a daze wandered up and down the aisles, dropping in cans and boxes. My list remained in my purse, so who knows what I'd find when I unloaded the sacks at home.

Get a grip, I scolded. *He'll be home over Thanksgiving, and besides, you'll see him in a few weeks when you visit the campus. Those other mothers saying good-bye are probably holding up better than you are.*

In the cereal aisle, I contemplated the many breakfast choices. I grabbed a box and stared at the ingredients and nutritional data, but my blurry eyes registered nothing. What of all those adages I'd read about giving your kids roots, then wings . . . about letting your children go? They were, after all, only on loan from God. I wondered when the author penned such wise thoughts—long before her children left home, or long after?

Just then something flitted by, and I noticed a floating string. I looked up and saw it was attached to a partly deflated, helium-filled balloon—probably loosed from its moorings in the floral department. Now it wandered lazily through the store, just overhead. Other shoppers didn't seem to notice.

I watched it float past, and something tugged at my heart. I looked long at the balloon and grinned. I knew its printed message—"I Love You"—was straight from God, a reminder that he was with me throughout this hard day. He had seen my mother-heart stretching to let go of my child, and he was reminding me of his Father-heart of love for his children. The message wrapped me in a hug. I thanked God for his kindness.

I focused on the cereal box in my hands, then I sighed and reshelved it—Adam was the only one who ate that brand.

I knew there would be rough days ahead, no question. Of course it was hard to let Adam go. But the bobbing balloon reminded me that God would be with me as I adjusted to the emptying nest. This was a season of life, and I would pass through it, guided, loved, and protected by my heavenly Father.

My Bible is full of I-love-you and I'll-always-be-with-you assurances, but God's love is enormous and personal enough that he sent a visible message—a helium promise right in the middle of the cereal aisle.

—Lynn Ludwick

ARE YOU THE ANGEL LADY?

I was only five miles from home, but I had no idea whether or not I was even going the right direction.

The fog that blanketed the world was truly as thick as pea soup the morning I insisted on driving across town to hold a scheduled home party for wickerware, a part-time job for me. My husband, Gary, didn't like the idea of my driving in the fog, but I felt we needed the money I would earn from doing the party.

The moisture hung so thick on the outside of the car that I kept my wipers at full speed. The moisture even seeped into the car, fogging the windshield inside and out. Because of poor visibility, I drove thirty-five miles per hour on the freeway and prayed no one would rear-end me.

Suddenly lights blinded me. Something blocked the road. I slammed on the brakes and felt my car slide, then jerk to a stop crosswise. The pickup behind me didn't stop. He drove around my car and slammed full force into the side of a jackknifed semitrailer.

An eerie silence hung suspended like the fog.

"Lady! You all right?" A man beat on my car window.

Crash! Crash! More cars smashed into the mess. None of them hit me.

"Lady, are you all right?" the guy demanded as he pulled on my door. "My semi jackknifed. Are you OK? I've got to check the others."

I nodded and watched him run away.

When I checked my car, I discovered that I was on a bridge, inches from the guardrail. Nothing had hit me. I had hit nothing. I stood amazed and shaken.

Lord, you protected me. I'm so stubborn. No one should be driving in this weather.

I stood there, not sure what to do next.

"Ma'am, the semi driver said you're OK. Can you help me?" The man who suddenly came through the fog didn't appear to be injured.

"My daughter . . ." He suddenly took off running toward his steaming pickup, and I followed. "What's your name?" The man yelled over his shoulder.

"Kathy Crawford." I don't know why I told him anything, but I did. "I live on Bertelsen Road. My husband is the pastor of Cornerstone Church."

"My name is Bill, and this is my daughter, Mary," he said as he lifted the child from the pickup. "Please take Mary to my wife."

He turned to his daughter and told her, "Honey, this is Mrs. Crawford. She's an angel lady and will take you back to Mama."

He carried the child to my car and buckled her in.

The man rattled off his life story as if we were best friends. He'd lost his job months before, was now almost bankrupt, and was on the verge of divorce. And now his pickup was totaled.

"She didn't want me out in this, but I insisted," he admitted. I knew exactly what Bill meant. "I can't leave until the police come. I can't thank you enough for taking Mary home."

"What is your wife's name?"

"Felicia." After giving me directions to his house, he shut my car door and walked toward the mangled metal that used to be his truck.

"Are you really an angel?" Mary asked me. Her opening sentence triggered enough conversation to guide us home— even though in the fog I got lost twice.

A police car sat in the driveway of his home by the time we arrived there. Felicia sobbed in relief. The police had called about the child coming with me. When they arrived ahead of me, Felicia was certain I'd kidnapped her child.

Inside the home, I noticed a bare Christmas tree in the corner of an almost empty living room. After I assured the officers of my integrity, they left. When the door closed, Felicia poured out her story—just as Bill had done—as if I were a counselor instead of the delivery lady.

In spite of my headstrong nature—or maybe because of it—I felt God had placed me in the middle of a family crisis.

I hugged Felicia and let her cry while I silently prayed, *Lord, what can I do for this family? We have no money. I thought today's wicker party might help our budget. Cornerstone is filled with street people. They don't have money. Lord, how can I help?*

"Someone gave us the tree, but we have no ornaments," Felicia said as she motioned to the beautiful green fir. "I know the kids can make stuff, but we don't have gifts. And now the accident."

When another officer brought Bill home, I excused myself with the promise to pray.

"You truly are an angel lady." Bill shook my hand.

At home, the shock of the morning hit me. While I sobbed like Felicia had done, Gary held me. The huge pileup didn't seem real, especially because I had driven away untouched.

"Hon, we have got to pray for all those people. From what Felicia said, they attended church before they had children," I insisted. So Gary and I prayed, repeatedly.

The next week I spoke at a large church in another city. The missionary society wanted to hear about our planter church. I talked about our baby Christians, the drug addicts, and the recovering alcoholics, and I also told them about Bill and Felicia.

After I spoke, a woman came up to me and said, "My committee wants to help."

She was true to her word. In a few days two vans and a car full of Christmas gifts, ornaments, clothing, household goods, and craft supplies arrived at our house.

Thanks to their generosity, Gary and I became Christmas angels. We delivered items to Cornerstone families and to Bill and Felicia.

I hoped the hurting couple might attend the Christmas services, but they didn't. Then one day the phone rang.

"Is this the angel lady?" I recognized Bill's voice. "Thank you again for helping us."

Bill gave me an update on the family. He'd found a job. They were still married. The kids were well. They'd enjoyed Christmas. "Best of all, we are in church again," he announced.

What an honor. God chose me to serve as his angel of mercy on one horrible foggy winter day, and he continues to receive the glory years later.

—Katherine J. Crawford

THE SPIRITUAL SIDE OF GOLF

"Are we having fun yet?" I asked my golfing partner as she stared at the ground.

"Well, I meant to hit the stupid ball a little farther," she muttered.

Her ball was buried in the dirt, the top barely visible.

"It looks to me like it's halfway to China or Australia. I forget which country is under us," I commented cheerily.

As Sharon struggled with her ball, I philosophized. "This is an opportunity to think about the spiritual side of golf," I said. "The beautiful thing about golf is that you can start over again each time you hit the ball. You can always have hope that next time you'll send it on its way exactly where you want it to go. Just like Christians when we make a mistake. We can ask forgiveness and start again from there. We don't have to keep rehashing our failures."

Sharon was not impressed by my spirituality as she dug her ball out of the dirt.

I smiled and said, "See, here's your chance to start fresh. Go ahead, you can do it."

She pointed to my ball. "Let's see how *you* do. There's no reason why I should be the only one to get the benefit of all this spirituality."

I was ready. As I had the right stance and the proper swing, each stroke should go right where I planned. My eyes were on the ball as I raised my club carefully and came down with all my might. I heard a sigh of relief from the ball as my club passed inches from where it lay. Clearing my throat, I said, "That was a practice swing. This time I'll hit the ball."

"Sure," she said. "What kind of spiritual analogy do you have for the letdown that comes when you miss the ball?"

"Um, let me think. I know there has to be one. Let's see, 'If at first you don't succeed . . .' No, that's not Scripture. How about, 'Claiming to be wise, they instead became utter fools'?" (Romans 1:22).

She laughed and said, "I'll accept that one."

My ball was pink, and it had "Flying Lady" printed on it. "Sandpit Sue" or "Tree-Climbing Theresa" would have been more appropriate. As I followed my ball to unexpected places, I discovered that golfing gives a person lots of time to contemplate these (and other) important things in life.

I've also learned that golfing amateurs generally compete against themselves. They hope their scores will be lower each time they play. However, a few people take golf a little too seriously. A group of ladies from my church decided to go golfing one afternoon. Cathy was in a group that golfed behind our group. Her group came in about forty-five minutes after we did. When Cathy finished, she was on fire to improve overnight.

"How did you like golf?" I asked.

"I loved it," she replied. "Just wait until next week. I'm getting a video and a coach. I'll leave you girls in my dust."

She was so enthusiastic I asked, "What was your score?"

Cathy sighed, "I got seventy-nine—"

"Wow, I'm impressed." I really was, until she continued.

"—on the first hole."

I tried not to sound superior. "You'll do better next time. Here's something you'll learn about scoring your game," I said. "It's like you were on a 1,200-calories–a-day diet. After you've reached your limit, you eat a piece of candy or a cookie, and something snaps. Suddenly, it doesn't matter anymore. You quit counting and start stuffing."

She looked confused as she asked, "And what does that have to do with my golf score?"

"I was just getting to that. You can get up to the green in two strokes. There's a little slant so you tap your ball ever so slightly with the putter. It rolls down the incline over the cup and keeps going. You shake your head in exasperation. *Oh well,* you think, *I'll sink this in four.*

"Now you have to nudge it uphill, so you have to use more oomph. This one rings the cup, hovers just long enough to give you hope, and spins away, out of control. All right, now it's getting frustrating. You're up to five and getting nowhere. After putting back and forth several more times, you finally get the ball to the cup, and it sits on the ledge. Figuring this is a gimme, you go to carefully plop it into the cup, and it rolls merrily away. You quit counting at ten, and when it finally drops in, you haven't a clue how many strokes you had."

In spite of these encouraging remarks, Cathy showed up the next week.

Out on the golf course we often discuss the beauty of God's creation and the way he's answered prayer. We reflect on how far we've come in our Christian walk and share ideas on the directions our lives are taking. Golfing has strengthened our friendship.

When one of us really belts the ball, everyone asks, "How did you do that?"

We answer, "I don't know." Then we spend the next hour trying to figure out what we did right.

One day out on the course, I realized that golfing is good for dieters. The candy bar in my hand made me think about it. Walking and dragging your cart is a great way to burn calories. And then you get extra mileage by retrieving lost items you drop along the way. Meanwhile, your golf partners are sidelined, waiting for you to return. The good news is you burn more calories than they did.

The most important thing about our group of golfing grandmas is that we have fun. We laugh together about our mistakes, and we rejoice when someone does something extraordinary. We feel blessed that we're able to be active and enjoy life. Golf is for all age groups—one sport that fits all. And I guess that's one last spiritual analogy of golf—the Christian life is for everyone, regardless of health, age, or background. When we know Jesus, faith, like golf, fits all.

—Midge DeSart

"Nancy, you're fired."

She used a euphemism—either "let go" or "laid off"—but it meant the same thing. I had seen it coming. I had struggled for months after a bad performance review. Meanwhile, God was giving me a different performance review: "You're not a businesswoman. You're in the wrong job; I have something better for you."

God had given me the courage and strength to face my boss. I even felt sorry for her because I knew it must be hard to fire someone. ". . . a man who will talk to you about what happens next," she was saying without looking at me, and she left the room.

The tall man who entered looked me straight in the eye and said, "You are not less because of what just happened."

I lost it. I could handle my boss's cool and businesslike manner, but this man's soft compassion undid me. I fought back tears, but they came anyway.

"There's something better for you," he said, echoing God's words to me. I suspected that he was a Christian, though he never came out and said so.

He told me about severance pay and the opportunity to receive help from a job outplacement service. I decided to take my time looking for a new job. I would go to the classes this service offered. The next day, I signed up for a general session where I'd learn more.

I also called Terri, the wife of one of our pastors. She had presented a class at our women's retreat a month earlier with the intriguing title, "PMS and loving it." The *P* was for passion, the *M* for mission, and the *S* for serving God. I knew she could help me spiritually as I thought about the future. For the next two months, I spent an hour a week with my spiritual counselor, Terri, and an hour with my business counselor.

In the business session, the instructor went around the room and asked us to tell where we had worked and where we thought we'd like to go next. I dreaded my turn: The others were there because their company had downsized.

"I was fired . . ." I began.

"Don't say that," the instructor interrupted. "They eliminated your job, right?"

I immediately pictured in my mind the girl half my age who was already doing my job. *Well, she could only do her job, not mine,* I rationalized, so I nodded.

"What else have you done?" she asked.

"I taught for fifteen years and proofread for four years before becoming an administrative assistant."

"What do you think you might like to do next?"

"I might want to try writing."

"You don't need a résumé for writing," she snapped.

"Teaching?" I offered reluctantly. Should I return to teaching after ten years? I had thought I was failing at teaching so I had gone into business.

"What are your skills and interests?" my instructor said,

interrupting my thoughts. I remained silent, unable to come up with anything.

"Teachers are compassionate," she said, writing on a board, "patient, caring, interested in helping others."

That sounded good. Did that describe me?

The next day, Terri informed me that before I could look at my future, I had to look at the past. That involved looking at what I considered to be a life of failure. Why had I struggled with teaching jobs? I had been "let go" three times. I saw that I had scrambled to take a new job as quickly as possible when one ended. I had made one bad choice after another, not willing to wait for the right job. Instead, I'd accepted positions teaching young teens—and I saw that I was not gifted at teaching young teens.

I began rewriting my history, my life story. No, not inventing new facts, but looking at the facts as God saw them. He did not see a failure but someone who had tried experiments that had not worked. He saw me trying to be someone I was not.

Hebrews 11 tells the stories of many men and women of faith. This version of their lives told just the "good stuff."

"It was by faith that Noah built a large boat to save his family from the flood. He obeyed God, who warned him about things that had never happened before. By his faith Noah condemned the rest of the world, and he received the righteousness that comes by faith" (Hebrews 11:7).

That passage doesn't mention that Noah overindulged in his vineyard after the flood (see Genesis 9:20-27).

"It was by faith that Abraham obeyed when God called him to leave home and go to another land. . . . He went without knowing where he was going. And even when he reached the land God promised him, he lived there by faith—for he was like a foreigner, living in tents. And so did Isaac and Jacob, who inherited the same promise" (Hebrews 11:8-9).

No mention is made of Abraham and Isaac, when they lied about their wives in order to save themselves—though they put their wives in peril (see Genesis 12:11-20; 26:6-10). The Scripture applauding them doesn't mention Jacob's deceiving his father (see Genesis 27:1-40).

Someday God will say to me, "Well done, good and faithful servant." And I am going to bite my tongue and not mention the "bad stuff"!

"Try rewriting your résumé. Try a different kind—a functional résumé," the instructor advised. I did not exclude any information, but focused on skills and abilities rather than the positions I'd held.

Meanwhile, Terri and I studied a list of spiritual gifts, and I wrote a spiritual résumé. I saw that God had indeed gifted me as a teacher. I had taught Sunday school, women's Bible studies, and small groups for many years. I often "left" teaching but came back. I learned that I needed to say no to anything that was not part of my passion, mission, or chosen way of serving God.

"What's your ideal job?" asked the instructor. I had loved one job: tutoring students in reading and writing skills at a college learning center. I had enjoyed working with international students, older adults returning to school, and inadequately prepared students who wanted to succeed in college. But that job had ended when the college closed the campus at the end of the semester. The other campuses did not have a tutoring program.

"Whom do you know?" This question about networking reminded me of two teachers. One was the head of the tutoring center where I had taught. I called him that afternoon.

"Sure, I'd be glad to recommend you for a job," he said, but he was no longer the director so he gave me the names of contacts. I never called them. I decided that I did not want to teach at a secular college.

The other teacher had been an elder in a church I had attended. Jim taught at a Christian school. I called him, too.

"Nancy—sure, I remember you!"

I told him I wanted to teach at a Christian college. "As long as you have a related master's degree, you could be an adjunct. Do you have one?" he asked.

"Yes, I do."

He gave me some addresses and phone numbers at the college. "Even if there's no opening now, send a résumé anyway. They are always looking for adjunct professors," he encouraged.

Although I was told in my class to send out one hundred résumés, I sent only two: one to a local community college and the other to the small Christian college forty miles away where Jim taught. Then I prayed and waited.

A month later, an administrator from another college— a school where Jim taught part-time—called me. I knew it was not the one for me, so I said, "No, it's too far."

The woman who called then made an interesting comment. "I know you'll be teaching at Jim's school next year, but I thought you might like to teach here until then."

"No," I said with confidence. This time I would wait and not make another wrong choice.

Sure enough, a year later I received a phone call from

the Christian college. "Are you still interested in teaching here?" the caller asked.

"Yes, I am," I said as calmly as my racing heart would let me. As the woman told me more, I realized God was answering my prayer even to minute details, such as having some free time to write.

A week later I signed a contract.

It was five years ago that I finally heard, "Nancy, you're hired."

—Nancy J. Baker

THE BRACELET BRIGADE

"You all left me alone, Mom!" My son's words stopped me in my tracks.

Ian was fifteen and quite capable of staying home alone for an afternoon. In fact, he often enjoyed having the chance to do as he liked without dealing with his sisters. This day, however, all three sisters left, in different directions. Dad worked while I attended a conference. Ian hadn't felt well enough to go with any of us.

Born with cystic fibrosis, Ian knew hospitalizations and treatments as a way of life. I was pretty sure he was ready for another fourteen-day visit with his favorite nursing staff. But this was Saturday. Ian had a regular doctor appointment scheduled for Monday, so he was hoping to hold out until the doctor visit.

I couldn't blame him. We'd experienced the lengthy emergency-room delay more than once. At this point in his young life, Ian had been admitted to the hospital more than thirty times. He was also quite stubborn, so I'd let him decide if he was feeling well enough to wait out the weekend.

Now I was starting to rethink that decision.

"Honey, do you feel like you should go to the hospital?"

"Mom, you guys all left me. That's what I'm upset about," he insisted as he pulled away from my touch.

"I'm sorry. I didn't think you'd be upset. In fact, I thought you'd enjoy having the house to yourself." I tried again to pull him to me. This time he didn't fight.

"I'm sorry too. I guess I just didn't think it'd be so long and boring." He sighed.

I ruffled his hair, which was finally growing out from his close cut. "Want to play some backgammon?"

"Yeah, but maybe you'd better check the messages, first."

That's strange, I thought as I picked up the phone. He'd never worried about checking messages before. Only one message waited on the phone, a young voice I did not recognize.

"I hope I have the right phone number. I am a friend of the Burkholders'. They asked me to call and let you know that Leslie died today, a little before 3:00 P.M. If you call me back, I will let you know about the services . . ." and she left her number.

I think my heart must have stopped at that moment. My mind rushed back to the last time I'd seen Leslie's smiling, eleven-year-old impish grin. She also had CF and had a huge crush on Ian. They had been in the hospital at the same time during his previous trip and had been discharged the same day—Ian to go home, and Leslie to head for California to begin the process of a lobar lung transplant. (Lobar transplants use two live donors, who each donate one lobe.) The family was to call us as soon as they had some word, but we hadn't heard a thing.

Until now.

The last thing I wanted to do was to tell my son his friend had died.

Ian took the message stoically. He had lost friends before, but I knew it got harder each time. Eventually, he tried not to get attached to other kids with CF, but Leslie was already his good friend. We'd nearly lost another close friend, Brian, a few months before. Brian was now at home on hospice care.

"Mom, why are my friends all sicker than I am?" Ian had asked me on the way home from the hospital, the day we'd said good-bye to Leslie. I'd had no answer. Now as I watched him struggle with Leslie's death, I knew he was remembering that question even though he didn't voice anything.

The next morning I called his doctor. After answering my page and hearing my concerns, he got on the phone with Ian and convinced him to go to the hospital, promising to have things ready so we wouldn't have to go through the ER. True to his word, a room was waiting, and the nurses, who seemed to wrap themselves around Ian's pinkie, were ready to help us get settled.

Leslie's service was the following Wednesday. I took time out to go. Her pastor shared how Leslie had put her faith in Jesus at a church camp the previous summer.

Linda, Leslie's mother, stopped by the hospital a couple of days after the service. She gave Ian a small, green, friendship bracelet after hearing that he, too, would be starting the lobar transplant process. Leslie had given the bracelet to her mother to wear until her transplant was complete. Now Linda wanted Ian to wear it.

Ian promptly put it on his thin wrist. "Do you think I should get Linda a bracelet, Mom?" he asked.

It was just like him to think that way. I told him I thought it was a good idea and asked what he wanted me to buy. "You'll know when you see it. I think it should be green. That was Leslie's favorite color."

Ian was right. I knew the right bracelet the moment I saw it. It was forest green and in the same style as the WWJD bracelets—only it spelled out FROG. The clerk explained it meant "Fully Rely On God." Perfect!

The next week, Linda came by, and Ian gave the bracelet to her. I could see that she was trying to hold back the tears as she told him she would never take it off—not even in the shower.

The fourteen days of Ian's hospitalization passed, and he was nowhere near ready to go home. This time the fight to get better was taking its toll on his fragile body. After one delicate surgery and three trips to the Intensive Care Unit, Ian went home to Jesus surrounded by his family and friends. Afterward, one of his favorite nurses brought me Leslie's bracelet. I vaguely remember slipping it on while loved ones hovered, trying to make sure we were all right.

But I wasn't all right. I was empty and numb. My sister and a close friend generously walked me through the next couple of days, and somehow the day of Ian's service arrived. Linda found me afterward, and we hugged and cried. I held up my arm with Leslie's bracelet on it, and she held up hers with Ian's.

"Do you want to trade back?" she asked, and I shook my head. I didn't know why, but somehow I knew that for now the bracelets were on the correct wrists.

A couple of weeks later, I began to feel something special might come of this. I wasn't sure what, but I found myself thinking about Ian's friend, Brian, who was still living at home on hospice care. I called Linda to see if she wanted to go with me to give Brian's mother, Vanessa, a bracelet.

She agreed, so again, I made the trip to the store, found one that said PUSH ("Pray Until Something Happens"), and had it beside me as I drove to meet Linda at Vanessa's home. But something wasn't right. It took almost until the moment I pulled in the driveway to realize that the bracelet wasn't for Vanessa. It was for Brian. Both Linda and I wore bracelets our children had worn. Brian had to wear this one.

Inside the house, we laughed and talked. Then came the moment to share the reason for our visit. I spoke directly to Brian as I told of how Linda and I had come by our bracelets. I also told him and Vanessa about one of Ian's last days when people had been visiting and praying for him. Ian had even worried that he wasn't being a very good host. Finally I explained to Brian, as I slipped the bracelet on his frail wrist, that it was to remind him to pray until something happened. Wise beyond his thirteen years, he nodded his head, and I gently hugged him.

Brian lingered for a few months more before Vanessa put the bracelet on her own wrist. She wears it still today.

While wearing the bracelets over the past few years, Linda, Vanessa, and I have tried to reach out to children in need. I volunteered at the schoolroom of Phoenix Children's Hospital. Linda helped at Leslie's school, and Vanessa began to work with the Special Education Department at Brian's school. In the summer of 2001, we were all together again with our husbands at a marriage retreat. It was good to laugh, cry, and catch up.

A couple of months after that, though, I began to realize I was heading into a dark depression. It seemed to deepen as the holiday season approached. Christmas had been a special time when Ian and I had always enjoyed decorating our house together. The Christmases without him had been hard, but this one was harder than the others.

I finally understood that I had not totally released Ian to God. I was trying to hang on to him, only to grasp at air. In the end, I prayed and told all this to God. As I released Ian into his care, I could feel the depression start to lift.

Now, a funny thing happened. That bracelet I had thought I would wear until the day I died suddenly felt like a tether. I looked at it and knew it would have to come off, but I wasn't ready. That was when we got the e-mail. Linda's husband had passed away after a sudden and short battle with cancer. I attended his service.

Afterward, as I waited to hug Linda, I knew it was time. She turned to me. "Stick out your arm," I said.

Silent questions in her eyes, she held out her arm, and I placed the bracelet, or what was left of it, on her wrist. "What's this?" she finally whispered.

"Leslie's bracelet." All the green covering was long gone, leaving only a white nylon cord. Linda embraced me, tears streaming down both our faces.

And just like that, I was free—free to finally realize I didn't need a bracelet, or manacle, as it ultimately had become, to hold on to Ian. He is in my heart and will always be until I hold him again in heaven. I can wait—and trust—resting in the knowledge I will, praise God, see him again.

—Jennifer Lynn Cary

LOOKING FOR BURIED TREASURE

"Just a little while longer," the woman pleaded. "There must be something more. My mother's jewelry box is here somewhere. All her rings and necklaces were in a small wooden box with beautiful hand-painted flowers on top. I know it's here. Please, just a little longer."

Our bodies had slowed considerably; aching, without a doubt, from the squatting and tedious rummaging we'd done for over six exhausting hours.

Five months after Hurricane Katrina destroyed endless miles along the Gulf Coast shoreline, twenty volunteers from my Midwest church traveled fifteen hours to Mississippi to help however we could.

One of the first people we met was a man who had originally intended to volunteer for a week, but after seeing the devastation, he quit his jobs back home and moved to the area to work full-time on the relief project. He acted as project manager to this particular "tent city"—an oversized, tent-covered dining hall that seated more than two hundred people and a second tent equipped with a full kitchen. He and his crew served three meals a day to at least five hundred hurricane victims and volunteers. The surrounding parking lot was filled with hundreds of pallets of food, water, and other items donated from around the country. The supplies, along with endless racks of clothing, were distributed twice a week to those in need.

During our first full day, he directed us to a job site that needed immediate attention. What had once been a lively oceanfront subdivision was now just desolate streets of rubble and ruin. Not one house was left standing for several blocks inland.

The property owners of one barren lot were thrilled to see us.

"Thank you so much for coming!" the woman's face beamed with appreciation.

"It means so much to us!" Her husband could hardly get the words out. The couple were covered with dirt and sweat and black mold smudges from the rotting remains. We surveyed a mountain of debris as they explained what they wanted done.

"We're digging through this pile," the woman said as she pointed to an enormous heap of what I would have easily mistaken for rubbish. "After sifting through it, we're bringing it over to this pile." She walked a few short yards to a second swell that stood only a couple of feet high. "I think if the men start dragging some of the bigger pieces out of the way, the ladies and I can sort through it to see what we can find."

Is this for real? I thought. *A Bobcat could do this in fifteen minutes.*

Before long the magnitude of this painstaking task took on a whole new meaning. We learned that the massive pile was not just the debris from one home but was actually three homes that had once stood side by side.

"So where is all the 'stuff'—the TVs, furniture, toilet?" we asked.

"Looters took most of it before we could get back into the neighborhood safely; anything they wanted, they took. If it could be hauled away, it was! Some of it might be lying in someone else's backyard somewhere," they answered with a laugh. "We found part of a refrigerator that came from three or four blocks away! All that's left now are things that don't mean much to anyone but us."

As the day passed, our feelings of sadness quickly turned to inspiration as we watched this couple. Every new find held a precious place in their hearts. We were delighted to discover a soiled toy and stopped momentarily to let the memory of their son receiving it for his fifth birthday engulf them. Off the woman would go to haul it to the "save" pile—her "treasures."

For most of the items we found that day, we had to ask if each was a "save" or a "toss." When we pulled something to save from the mess and they told us its story, we shared in their joy and laughter rang throughout the group. We must have looked pretty strange to onlookers: twenty people down on all fours, sifting through one bucketful of debris at a time, then cheering as we pulled out a single strand of Mardi Gras beads still intact.

We learned so much about the family that afternoon. They had two boys who are now adults but had grown up in the house. They had played Little League and soccer and had taken piano lessons, just like my own kids had. The man collected coins and had too many remotes, and the woman liked bright red fingernail polish and Beanie Babies. They knew that most of this stuff would find its way to the trash eventually, but right then, it was nice to have a few bits and pieces to hold on to.

When you arrive home from a trip like that, you see your life from a whole new perspective. I'd like to believe that I was changed by my experience—not just for a short time but in a way that will affect me the rest of my life.

I had to take a second look at my treasures. Did they hold special meaning, and could I recall the heartfelt story behind them? Or were they just things that cluttered my house and could easily be forgotten if they were carried away by looters? I wondered if I was taking time to enjoy our family, or was I too busy to stop and enjoy the memories?

I believe sometimes things happen that allow us to step back and take a second look at ourselves. God used our group that week in a memorable servant role, but I believe we were the ones who received the blessing. He used the situation to help me readjust my own life. He taught me to focus more on friends and family than on "stuff."

Sometimes life isn't good, but God is still great. He can take a horrible, devastating situation and somehow bring people together, bless them, and strengthen their love for others in our world.

—Jennie Hilligus

DOWN WITH DOILIES

We vowed we'd never be pink doilies. My friend Heidi and I attributed the title "pink doilies" to women who seemed to do it all—especially activities we saw as having very little to do with Christlike discipleship.

Pink doilies whip up dinner for twelve faster than a speeding bullet; are more powerful than a locomotive, with five bags of groceries in one arm and a powdered, diapered, and nursing baby in the other; and are able to leap mounds of children in a single bound to chide one for smacking his sister. They crochet and knit at the same time, are successful businesswomen, and mow the lawn while tending the fattest and finest flowers in the neighborhood. They have the best-behaved children in church, husbands with the widest grin, the cleanest house, and the neatest hairdo. And they do it all without ever breaking a sweat or a well-manicured nail.

Nope. We swore off them and their pink-doily ways forever. No pink doilies for us, we cried! We thought ourselves to be Marys, down at Jesus' feet, instead of Marthas, preparing dinner for a crew of twelve and complaining that their sisters weren't helping (see Luke 10:38-42). We'd settle for messier homes, overgrown lawns, fading flowers, and last decade's hairstyle for a little peace, quiet reflection, and creativity. And we guaranteed we'd probably sweat doing even that!

So when my husband started down the road to becoming a pastor, I offered my congratulations and my trepidation. Pastor's wives, I decided, were the ultimate pink doilies—Martha times ten. My husband would be in trouble.

"I'm not sure I'm going to make a very good pastor's wife," I said, my preconceived notions of a pastor's wife wreaking havoc on my self-esteem as I planned my family's Thanksgiving dinner. "I don't play the piano, I'm not a children's Sunday school teacher, I don't direct plays, and I certainly can't organize a Sunday brunch for an entire congregation while trying to remember who's in the hospital. I'm not a pink doily."

After I later explained *pink doily* to him, he tried to reassure me that surely no congregation would expect its pastor's wife to do all this. But as I finished knitting the fifteen scarves for friends and family for Christmas, I insisted. Even our denomination's pastoral licensing application seemed to drive pastors' wives toward dreaded acts of pink doilyism. It asked (no—accused!) whether I played the piano or if I sang. And though it didn't ask if I could direct the children's Easter pageant, I already saw the disaster in my mind: petals from Easter lilies strewn about the altar; children running to and fro, halos askew, to the horror of hundreds of pew-covering parents; me yelling, "Grab that donkey!" at the top of my lungs.

My husband wasn't only in trouble, he was doomed! A pastor without a pink doily at his side—he'd be handicapped, a black sheep, a laughingstock! After all, his wife was a Mary, not a Martha.

As time passed and the denomination's licensing committee picked its way through my husband's application, I continued my protest. My resistance became even louder as the time approached for the two of us to meet with the licensing committee.

"I am a professional," I told my husband, as I shoved another baking sheet of raw cookie dough into the oven for our church's choir and cookie night and mopped the kitchen floor for the third time that month. "I am a writer! I do not have a cake-baking degree from the University of Baked Delights!"

My husband only smiled and reminded me I should have an open heart about helping out in areas where a future church might need me. This was not the response I wanted. Crestfallen, I turned to Heidi, my non–pink-doily partner in crime.

After explaining the color motif I'd planned for the guest room in my house, I bemoaned my situation. How would I ever fit in, I asked Heidi. What if I'm not at church on a Wednesday evening with my husband? What if we never had children so I wouldn't relate to other mothers in the congregation? I'm more interested in theology and apologetics than in trying to teach Stormie Omartian's *The Power of a Praying Woman*. On top of that, I'm a jeans and T-shirt kind of woman—they couldn't expect me to dress in frilly skirts or suits every Sunday!

"So you won't be the typical pastor's wife," Heidi told me. I'd break the mold. Congregations shouldn't expect their pastors' wives to be perfect pink doilies. I knew she'd understand. Vindicated, I launched into an exposition about planning a brunch for the Sunday school class my husband taught.

The day before we met with the denomination's licensing committee, I headed to Dress Barn to find a new outfit for the occasion, while thinking about the dreaded question, "Do you play the piano?"

After we arrived the next day, we exchanged pleasantries with the committee and sat around square tables arranged so we could all see one another. While they asked my husband to explain theological minefields, I knew they were simply biding their time, waiting to find out what I could possibly offer a church congregation.

So, you can't play the piano, I could hear them ask in my mind, *and you can't sing. What exactly* can *you do? Can you at least cook?*

My palms sweat. My stomach fluttered. My mouth felt like an arid desert.

But the question never came. Instead, they asked how I felt about the application process and whether I confirmed my husband's heart for the ministry. But I knew what they were thinking. Deep down, that question—*What exactly does she do?*—swirled.

After the meeting, they shook our hands, thanked us for coming, and said they'd be in touch. We weren't sure where we stood. It seemed like the meeting went smoothly, but their faces revealed nothing about which way they'd vote. We waited.

As the weeks turned into months, busyness overtook me. My work flourished, and I all but forgot about pink-doily pastors' wives as I volunteered and planned a baby shower for my sister-in-law, who was expecting her first child—a little girl—in a few months. I baked cupcakes with pink frosting, turned my kitchen table into a welcome center for women

I'd never met, planned silly baby-shower games, made pink sorbet punch, blew up balloons, and made party favors—pink-and-white baby shoes out of tiny plastic cups.

As I was cutting into my twentieth plastic cup, my husband looked over my shoulder at the plastic baby shoes filled with candy for the guests.

"Aren't they adorable?" I said.

"Yes," he said. "But isn't that a little bit pink doily?"

I turned and glared. *No!*

"For not being pink doily, you do a lot of pink-doily stuff," he said. He pushed: "You knit, you keep the house spotless, you're a good cook, you paint pottery . . ."

My scissors stopped in midchop. I looked down at what I'd created: rows and rows of little plastic baby shoes filled with candy for baby-shower guests. The horror of it all etched on my face. I remembered the scarves I'd knit, the rooms I'd painted with modern color schemes, the pottery I'd decorated, and I knew it was true. I could deny it no longer. Except for the powdered, diapered, and nursing baby over my shoulder, I had to finally admit my pink-doily tendencies. And it dawned on me: Just call me Martha.

In the end, the committee licensed my husband to be a pastor. And since then, I've been learning what it really means to sit at Jesus' feet.

—Jennifer Ochstein

FROZEN DREAMS AT
HEARTLAND LODGE

When I drove up and down the steep hills on the three-mile stretch of gravel road toward our beautiful Heartland Lodge that Friday morning, I had a lot on my mind. A wedding party had booked the entire lodge for the whole weekend. It was the first wedding we'd host since the lodge had been built just fifteen months earlier, and I wanted everything to be perfect.

The wedding rehearsal and dinner would be that night, followed by brunch Saturday morning, with the wedding in the afternoon. Then on Sunday, we'd prepare another big meal before the wedding party and guests departed.

As I drove to the lodge from my home forty miles away, I couldn't believe how cold it was. The temperature was a few degrees below zero, with a windchill factor of twenty-five below zero—unheard of cold for southern Illinois. As I slowed down on the steep hills that led to the lodge, I made a mental list of everything we needed to do to get ready for the rehearsal dinner.

I turned into the circle drive and noticed a few more things to add to my list: *Shovel the snow on the driveway. Throw salt on the sidewalks. Remove the ladder from the front porch. Unpack the decorations for the wedding.*

When I opened the door to the lodge to begin the final preparations for the big weekend, an eerie steam cloud engulfed me. It felt like I'd walked into a sauna. The floor was covered with two inches of water! I heard water running from everywhere, an ugly hissing sound gushing out of the pipes.

I could only stand there, waving my arms. "Oh my goodness! Oh my goodness! Oh God, please help me!"

Immediately a feeling of peace came over me. In my head, clear as a bell, I saw the organized, framed list of water pipes and their locations. When the lodge was finished the previous October, I'd asked our contractor to give me a diagram of everything in the water and furnace room so I'd know how to get things fixed if we encountered a problem. He had typed a neat list of all the pipes and where they were located and then numbered each pipe with the corresponding number on the framed sheet. I raced down the stairs to the recreation room and over to the furnace room. I had to shut off the water before the entire lodge flooded!

On that long list, the main water valve was #1. As I turned around to look at the maze of pipes all over one wall, I shouted, "Oh God, please help me find valve #1! Please, God . . . !"

Immediately, I turned around and walked to the opposite corner of the little room, and there in bold red letters on a handle on one of the pipes was "#1." Using every ounce of strength I had, I turned and turned that handle until the water shut off and the awful sound of rushing water was silenced.

I looked around the lodge. Ceiling tiles in our beautiful new recreation room and downstairs bedrooms were wet, had fallen to the floor in soupy puddles of Styrofoam and water, and had broken. The plush burgundy carpets in the halls, bedrooms, and rec room were sopping. The beds downstairs were soaked. Elegant draperies, bedspreads, lace-trimmed sheets, and blankets were drenched.

Oh, my beautiful lodge! How could this have happened?

Just over a year earlier, our family had opened the doors to Heartland Lodge for the first time. We'd lived away from the country for thirty years, and I wanted to get back to my roots, to the serenity and beauty of this land where my husband, Gary, and I grew up. We had talked it over with our two grown children, and we all agreed to build a lodge on the thousand acres of land bordering the farm that had been in my family for more than one hundred years. We wanted to share the wooded hills, valleys, trails, and ridges on our land in Pike County with everyone—strangers and friends alike.

In just three months, the contractor we'd hired built our beautiful 7,500-square-foot lodge out of solid oak logs. It was large enough to hold thirty people, with thirteen bedrooms. Using ideas from friends and neighbors, we built a place rustic enough to allow a tired, flannel-shirted deer hunter to relax after a long day in the woods, yet beautiful enough for a couple to find an elegant country respite from the stress of city life.

My daughter, Stephanie, and I filled the lodge with exquisite furnishings—everything from extra-long, luxury-sheeted beds; feather pillows; plush carpet; and comfy leather sofas and chairs to the rustic artwork; Remington horse sculptures; and stuffed deer, turkey, bear, otter, and fish. It was all part of our plan to create a lodge so comfortable that strangers who came to enjoy the beauty of our land would leave as friends.

Now, as I surveyed the damage done by the broken

water pipes, I could think of only one person—that sweet bride who was trusting us with not only her rehearsal and the dinner that night but also with her wedding the next day and the festivities after that.

No way am I going to disappoint her, I kept telling myself. *Oh God, help me. I need you, heavenly Father.*

As soon as the housekeepers, Joyce and Becky, stepped in the front door just after I'd arrived, I sent them back home to collect their Shop-Vacs. Next, I called the contractor who'd built the lodge for us. "Gerald, you have to come out here right away. We have a terrible mess. And the whole lodge is booked for a wedding starting tonight. I need you to get this place back the way it was . . . by four o'clock this afternoon, Gerald!"

"Wanda, don't you worry. I'll call all ten of my men back from their other jobs, and we'll be out there. We'll do what we can."

"Gerald, we can't ruin this bride's wedding. I'll get more helpers in here, and we'll get the water soaked up and get the linens dried," I outlined. "You fix the pipes and the ceiling. Bring some fans, please—lots of fans. We'll have to dry the carpets and the mattresses."

I walked to the kitchen. The beautiful oak floor was underwater and was starting to buckle. The hallways and two bedrooms upstairs were drenched.

I made more phone calls to friends and neighbors, asking for help. I called professional carpet cleaners. I phoned Jason, a seventeen-year-old friend of ours who'd done odd jobs for us. He drove forty miles on dangerous, icy roads to help us all day. Joyce and Becky told other friends about our dilemma and then got busy putting plastic bags under the legs of all the furniture so none of the pieces would be ruined by sitting in the water. They ran Shop-Vacs all morning, then arranged to have food brought out for all the workers.

More and more people arrived to help, including some people I barely knew. I called two dry-cleaning establishments to see if I could bring in all the bed linens and draperies to be cleaned by 4 P.M. "Sure thing, Mrs. Harpole. We'll put everything else aside and take care of it today."

Later that morning when the county road crew heard about our disaster and about the wedding, they came out and cleared the roads of snow. Roger, our neighbor, cleared our long driveway and the circle drive in front of the lodge.

Because the water was turned off all day, Cheryl, my chief cook, couldn't begin to prepare the big rehearsal dinner until the very last minute. It didn't seem to faze Cheryl, however, because she was too busy helping clean up the water mess. As soon as the water was turned on late that afternoon, Cheryl dropped everything and cooked up a storm. She went from one job to the next without a flap or a fluster.

Throughout that long day, I flitted upstairs and downstairs, from room to room, answering questions and helping where I could. Our son, who had moved back to the family farm after college and was the one who actually helped turn our lodge dreams into reality, came out immediately and started working. So many friends, neighbors, and workers from all over the county helped out that I couldn't believe the miracle before me.

By five o'clock that afternoon, the lodge was dry, pipes fixed, ceiling tiles replaced, linens cleaned, and dinner ready for the eighteen wedding-rehearsal guests. The wedding the next morning was stellar, the bride a vision of loveliness.

In fact, all weekend she kept telling me, "Everything is just perfect."

I had never understood that God takes care of me, Wanda, on a personal basis every day until the day the lodge flooded. Until then, I thought I was self-sufficient and could take care of anything or anybody. But I learned that day, amid the flurry of people who inundated our lodge with helping hands, that God has no hands except those of friends, neighbors, relatives, coworkers, and strangers. And on that cold, wind-chilled day in January, I saw God in the faces of dozens of people and experienced his provision through their willing hands.

—Wanda Harpole, as told to Patricia Lorenz

RIGHT HERE, DAD

For a few minutes when he picks up the phone to answer it, Dad seems just the same. "And a good morning to you," he'll say in his cheerful, singsongy greeting. And then he slips, like a vapor, into confusion, hurrying to get the phone to my mom to let her carry on the conversation.

How much longer will he even recognize me, I wonder?

Lately, his decline has been rapid. The first few years, the decline was slow— hardly noticeable. Back then, we saw a few hints of trouble, but our need to believe Dad was OK trumped reality and good sense.

My parents live about an hour away from my home so I don't see them that often. A few years ago, I noticed changes in my dad. Tip-of-the-tongue-itis, for one thing. But I figured that wasn't really so unusual for a seventy-five-year-old. What was more disconcerting was that Dad often said he was expecting a windfall. "Any day now, Suz!" he would whisper, brown eyes sparkling.

One day, my brother called with alarming news. Stopping by my parents' house, he'd noticed a bundle of yellow Western Union receipts on Dad's desk. Curious, he did some amateur detective work and discovered that Dad had been the victim of a Canadian sweepstakes scam—actually, more than one. The receipts totaled the staggering sum of one hundred thirty-five thousand dollars. Even more horrifying, Dad was wiring money to these con artists from the home-equity line, jeopardizing my parents' financial security. Once we knew that our parents were two elderly people in need of intervention, my siblings and I dropped everything and sprang into action to protect them. My mother had realized something was wrong with Dad but didn't know what to do. She'd always relied on Dad; the sudden role reversal overwhelmed and incapacitated her. Our parents ended up having to sell their home and move into an independent retirement community.

We hoped that strange episode in my dad's life was behind him, like an odd blip on the radar screen. At least, for now, they were safe.

Soon, though, my dad seemed to lose interest in his activities. He had always been heavily involved in volunteer work at the church, but not any longer. He just didn't seem to care anymore. He stopped reading books or watching the news each evening. Bossing my mom became his only pastime: "Hurry up! We have to get home!" he would scold her crossly, embarrassing her in public and at family get-togethers.

Truth be told, my dad has always been in a hurry, but he has never been unkind. The main focus of his life has been to make a contribution. The list includes being a World War II veteran, the captain of the track team at his elite East Coast college, a husband and father of four, a small-business owner, and an elder of his church. Without exaggeration, he was one of the most generous men you could ever hope to meet.

Dad's finer qualities were not obvious to other people at the retirement community, but unfortunately, his newer and less-admirable qualities were. Before long, the administrators of the retirement community started calling my siblings and me to attend uncomfortable assessment meetings. They had a long list of resident complaints about Dad's behavior: thrusting his hands into the salad bowl in the buffet line, obsessively collecting recycled cans in resident wings that he didn't belong in, riding his bike through the hallways, scaring other residents.

Who was this person they were complaining about? How could that possibly be my dad?

Once again, we hauled Dad to the doctor's office. After many more tests and visits to specialists, it was declared that Dad most likely had early stages of Alzheimer's disease.

What a cruel end to a life well lived. As Alzheimer's disease claims Dad's mind, we are watching his personality slip away, along with his vocabulary and life skills. Just the other morning, I took him to the grocery store because he needed a new comb. In his hand, he held some coins, but he could not connect the price of the comb to those coins in his hand. What must it be like for him to live in a fog of confusion? No wonder he is easily frustrated.

Almost cruelly, his body remains quite robust. Eventually, as the disease progresses, brain cells will die and his body functions will fail him too. And he will require total care—exorbitantly expensive, twenty-four-hour care.

Alzheimer's is a disease with a voracious appetite. According to the Alzheimer's Association, an estimated 4.5 million Americans have Alzheimer's disease. The number of Americans with Alzheimer's has more than doubled since 1980, and it continues to grow. By the year 2050, the number of individuals with Alzheimer's could range from 11.3 million to 16 million.

But this individual isn't just a statistic. This is my dad! How can God let something like this happen to someone like my dad? Where is God in the midst of Alzheimer's disease? There is no way to fix this; medication might slow the decline a bit, but this illness marches ahead, completely out of our control.

One day in a doctor's office, I absently read the Serenity Prayer tacked up on the green wall of the sterile waiting room. "Lord, help me to accept the things I cannot change," it recommended. Things like the mess Alzheimer's makes of a person's life. Things like the strange loss we feel as the father and grandfather we all love disappears—though his body remains. Things like the financial worries that gnaw away at us as we try to take good care of Dad and find good care for him.

I read it again: "Help me to accept the things I cannot change."

OK, God, I silently prayed, *you win. I'm going to let go of the whys and trust you to help us get through this, at each and every stage.*

That very evening, I picked up *Blue Shoe* by Anne Lamott, in which the main character, Mattie, copes badly with her mother's decline into dementia.

In the book, one night Mattie asked her boyfriend, "Why would a loving God take everything away from my mother?"

The boyfriend replied, "I don't see that God is taking anything away from her. I see him taking care of her, instead: It's her illness that has done all the taking."

That hit me between the eyes, hard. God hasn't disappeared; he isn't missing. There are blessings in the midst of this trial. My brothers and sister and I have never been closer.

We have shared this burden in a remarkable way, each taking responsibility for areas in which we are best suited to help.

We've encountered other blessings too. It is a blessing to be needed, even if it doesn't always feel that way. My faith is expanding as I discover other dimensions of God's trustworthiness. He keeps providing just-in-time answers to prayers. And I mean just in time. I have found that God seems to have a fondness for eleventh-hour answers. Often slow, in my earthly judgment, but never late.

Just this week, Dad didn't recognize Mom for the first time.

"Where is Barbara?" he asked, looking right at her. "We have to go find her."

"Joe, I'm right here," she answered, poignantly aware of the significance of his question.

But her simple response isn't simple. It's profound.

We're all right here, Dad. So is God. His promise is true: "I will not fail you or abandon you" (Joshua 1:5).

—Suzanne Woods Fisher

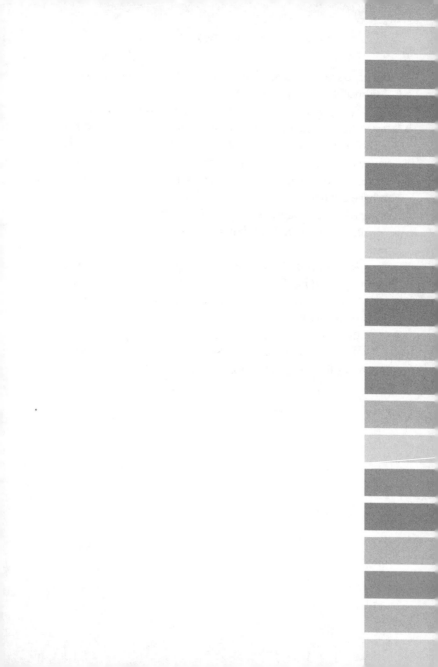

NANA CAMP

Hannah lived with us for several years after her birth. Her grandpa and I loved being part of her life as she grew from a cute toddler to an active and bright schoolgirl. When Hannah was able to move back with her mom, our feelings were mixed, enjoying the quiet of our home but missing her chatter and questions.

Hannah liked her new stepfather and his kids, but she missed the focused attention and activities she had grown accustomed to at our house. The long, hot days of summer vacation dragged by, with the children caring for themselves during the day while their parents were at work. Though this was perfectly safe and couldn't be helped, I felt sorry they had no one to give them attention or take them places.

Then one morning my feelings gelled into an idea.

"I can take the kids somewhere every week!" I exclaimed at breakfast. "I'll call it Nana Camp!"

My husband looked at me quizzically, then smiled as I explained my plan.

Our first venture was the next week. "What time shall I pick you up Thursday?" I asked Hannah and her stepsiblings. "We'll be going to the botanical garden."

"Garden?" twelve-year-old Darryl muttered. "What's there to do at a garden?"

"It'll be fun if Nana's there!" Hannah responded loyally.

"It's summer and I sleep late," fourteen-year-old Dee said. "I'm not up till ten o'clock."

"I can be there about eleven," I suggested. "I think we'll have fun!"

"Well, it'll be better than just sitting around the house all day," Dee answered without enthusiasm.

The Missouri Botanical Garden was showcasing a Dale Chihuly exhibit.

"'Glass in the Garden'?" Darryl read from the sign. "Give me a break!"

Then the children saw the amazing creations from Chihuly's studio.

"Wow! That's awesome!" Darryl admitted.

After the glass exhibit, they happily got lost in the maze and fed the koi ("radical big fish!"). Darryl went up a tree, and the girls admired the multihued roses.

"Thanks, Nana!" Hannah said, giving me her usual tight hug at the end of the day. Dee and Darryl just walked into the house, but their smiles betrayed their enjoyment of the activity.

"I can run faster than a T. rex," Hannah called the next week as we walked into the St. Louis Science Center.

"I'm gonna climb that rock wall," Darryl said, and up he went.

Again, at the end of the day, Hannah gave me a big hug and a heartfelt, "Thank you, Nana!"

And again, Dee and Darryl had nothing to say.

"Watch me jump in the deep end, Nana!" Hannah shrieked the next week.

A swimming pool is a real blessing in the heat of a St. Louis summer. The children and I splashed and jumped and laughed.

Suddenly Dee called out, "Hey! Hey! Look at Nana!"

The slide looked like so much fun, I just couldn't resist. Down I swooped, laughing, as the children cheered.

"Pretty cool!" Darryl agreed.

Back at the house, Dee said softly, "Thanks, Nana," before going into the house.

Next we went to Made By Me, a huge craft place. Each of us selected something to make from leather, beads, paint, and ceramics. In following weeks, we went bowling, rode the paddleboats in Forest Park, played every video game you can imagine at Dave & Buster's, saw a marionette show, and rode a carousel. We went fishing and had a picnic.

"Can I call you Granny?" Darryl asked one hot afternoon. "That's the name I like."

"Well, sure!" I agreed, touched.

Darryl was carrying the camera as we hiked through a small woods.

"Oh!"

I wondered why his voice showed such gentleness and awe until I, too, spotted the young rabbit nibbling clover. Darryl crept closer, every movement small and quiet. He stopped to snap a picture of the little animal, then moved to the side and took another.

"I think you took a million pictures of that bunny!" I said with a laugh as I dropped the kids off at the end of the day.

"I sure did!" Darryl exclaimed. "Thanks, Granny!"

He accepted my hug and ran into the house grinning.

My grin was pretty big too.

Darryl loved all wildlife. On our jaunts he took a "million pictures" of the great heron we saw from the paddle-boats and "another million" of the river turtle found in my backyard.

Some weeks we stayed home, baking and decorating cookies, getting out board games such as Sorry, or playing volleyball in the backyard.

"Be nice," Dee cautioned Darryl, who was getting ready to serve the ball during a volleyball game. "Remember, Hannah's only eight, and Nana's pretty old."

Darryl served, and I spiked the ball over the net.

"Whoo-hoo! Way to go! You're not a too-old Nana!"

As we planned for the next week, Darryl asked, "Hey, can we go to the movies?"

"Of course," I said. "Remember, Hannah's too little for PG-13 shows, though."

The kids scanned the paper for interesting movies.

"That's PG-13."

"That's a baby movie!"

"That sounds boring!"

"I've seen that one!"

"You know, we can do something else if you'd rather," I suggested, beginning to fear they would never be able to agree on a show.

But they really wanted to go, so they kept talking and arguing and suggesting and coaxing until they came to an agreement.

"You guys did a good job of working out that problem," I pointed out to them. "You communicated well, took turns, and nobody got mad—well, not too mad! That was good problem solving!"

"You sound like a teacher," Darryl observed.

"Well, call it a Nana lecture," I said as I laughed.

The kids laughed too. After that I felt free to interject "Nana lectures" on such topics as choosing your friends rather than letting them choose you, or the importance of waiting till God reveals the right spouse and not rushing into relationships just because they feel good. I kept these talks short, and the children took them with a good spirit.

"Here comes another Nana lecture!" they might announce. But they were listening, and I hoped I was planting seeds that would help shape their futures.

One day Hannah asked wistfully, "Nana, can we spend the night?"

So one week we had a sleepover, with pancakes for breakfast in the morning. Even Dee got up early when she smelled the bacon and maple syrup.

I even carted the kids with me that summer to the Christian family camp my family attends each August in Wisconsin. This year Dee and Darryl came along because they were definitely part of the family. What fun for city kids to spend a week playing and learning in the woods! And how much I enjoyed being with them as they did it!

When the summer was over, I made a personalized photo album for each child to help him or her remember our time together. Of course, we featured Darryl's "millions" of animal pictures. On the last page, I included a character trait that I appreciated and a Scripture verse—different for each.

A friend of mine pointed out, "That's a lot of effort for

two kids who aren't even related to you and who are at an awkward age!"

I guess it might appear that way. But I'm already thinking about next summer's Nana Camp. What started as an outreach by me ended by God blessing me with some wonderful new "grandchildren," a deeper relationship with my own precious Hannah, and a more exciting summer than I've had in a while—full of adventures and exercise, challenging conversations, and more love than I knew how to give or receive.

When I was a child and someone asked me what I wanted to be when I grew up, I knew I just wanted to be a mother. That part of my life has long passed, but God enabled me to thrive as a grandmother this past summer. My cup overflows.

—Anne Agovino, as told to Elsi Dodge

A CADILLAC BLOUSE IN
A JOHN DEERE WORLD

There it was: a Cadillac blouse in a John Deere world.

My very own "John dear" lovingly decided to do his laundry while I was out of town. Perhaps needing something to fill out his load of old jeans and muddy gardening togs, he spotted my new, 100 percent silk, Liz Claiborne blouse in the special place I'd put it to carefully hand wash.

To my horror, when I got home and started on the housework, I opened the dryer door to discover my pure silk, soft-peach blouse peeking out through the heap of dark, heavy, manly clothes, much like a delicate rose among thorns.

The dial indicated they had been roasted together on "High." All the clothes had that weathered, Mojave Desert look about them that says, "Help me! I've been braving scorching winds and blazing sun for as long as I can remember, and if someone doesn't rescue me, I'm go . . . *hack—sputter—gag* . . . I'm g . . . I'm . . ."

Courageously, I held up my once-beautiful blouse to find it had not only changed color but sported a large irreparable rip in the front as well. In some bizarre way, I could imagine what that blouse would have felt if it had feelings. Maybe you can imagine it too. We often find ourselves thrown mercilessly into a crowd of divergent folks—not necessarily *better* or *worse*, just *different*. We ponder the proverbial whys and hows of our lives: *Why am I here? How can I cope?* And in desperate times, we even consider the wheres: *Where is the eject button?*

If you're a city girl married to a farm boy or a farm girl married to a city boy, you know that feeling every time you're surrounded by the other's kinfolk.

A thousand people could give a thousand different examples of a time they felt like the Lone Ranger at Tonto's family reunion. Maybe you've been the resident "grandmother" in a freshman college class . . . the only nondrinker at a public school or secular college class reunion . . . a Christian working among avowed atheists . . . a single at a couples' event . . . a political conservative in a study group of radical liberals.

Sometimes the out-of-place feeling enters even the four walls we call home. I knew a petite mom, the lone female in a houseful of burly guys who would teasingly pick her up and carry her wherever they wanted her to be. I knew a dad, the token male in a houseful of girls—he'd sit patiently waiting by the door while they sorted out last-minute crises such as missing purses, borrowed-sweater disputes, hairdo hassles, and outfit changes.

What about our Lord Jesus Christ? Can any of us begin to imagine what it must have been like for God the Son to come to earth to become the Son of Man? to choose to trade his kingly robes for an earthly one? to dine with and rub shoulders with, to minister to and commiserate with, to serve and save, to love and walk among the likes of . . . us?

You and I will have those moments when we feel isolated in a crowd—a crowd divided, often inadvertently, by age, culture, gender, political persuasion, or lifestyle. Yet we are called to survive in those situations, even expected to thrive in them. How?

In *Daughters of Promise,* Christine Wyrtzen's daily devotional (see April 15, 2007), she expresses simply, beautifully, what the Lord might answer: "Learn to hide yourself away with Me, not only during our private times but in the midst of a crowd. In doing so, you will be oblivious to others' reactions to you. You will only know the joy of My still, small voice. No longer will you be obsessed with the acceptance of friends and family."

I remember the day God first called me to put this into action. I was a young Christian, "alone in a crowd" of cousins who had recently been added to my family album. On this beautiful afternoon, I was enjoying getting acquainted with these fine folks until they began to launch into party mode around the barbecue pit. As they became increasingly inebriated and offensive, I became increasingly uncomfortable and afraid. I slipped away, unnoticed, to my car twenty yards away.

Amid the sounds of revelry, I sat in the passenger seat, clutching my New Testament to my chest. With the warmth of the sun's rays streaming through the sunroof and tears rolling down my face, I cried out, "Lord, show me how to do this. Jesus did it so well. I want to be a light, not a judge, among these you've called me to love. . . . I need you to show me . . . please."

God's still, small voice spoke to my heart, giving me words of peace and encouragement, and assuring me I need not feel alone in the crowd or crave their acceptance. I was to live this very moment "in the refuge of his love," and he would take it from there.

And he did.

So how about you? Have you been thrust into a "load of overalls" lately, feeling a bit overwhelmed, alone, or afraid?

The peach-colored blouse had emerged the worse for wear, but we don't have to. If we choose to hide in him, we can be the better for it—even better than if we'd remained cloistered in a "delicates only" pile. For it's in the harsh realities of life that we come to best appreciate the beauty of his special care.

—Sandi Banks

"What is that in your hand?"

When I heard that quote from Exodus 4:2 for the third time in two days—in my morning devotional, on the radio, and in a sermon—I figured that maybe God was trying to get my attention.

That Scripture refers to Moses' experience at the burning bush when God asked him, "What is in your hand, Moses?"

God had a lesson for Moses to learn and a job for him to do. I'm sure Moses didn't feel he was very well equipped for the job God had just given him. After all, he had only his shepherd's staff in his hand. It may have been a good, stout stick with which he guided his sheep and scared off predators, but still it was just an ordinary tool. And God wanted him to lead half a million people out of slavery in Egypt into the desert. He would have to provide everything they needed until they got to the land that God had promised his ancestors would someday belong to them. There would be no McDonald's every few miles.

Moses, once before in his idealistic youth, had tried to correct the injustices he witnessed among the Israeli slaves. He had not been very successful and had ended up running for his life into this desert where he had been hiding for forty years.

Instead of being part of the royal family with privileges,

authority, and Pharaoh's ear, now he was a menial laborer working for his father-in-law, with a wife and family to support. He still worshiped God, but he did not expect anything special from God as he went about his daily business.

Kind of like me.

At one time in my idealistic youth, I wanted to do great things for God, such as going to Bible college and serving him in exotic places. But that was not how my life turned out. I married a handsome young man and immediately began a family. Over the next twenty years, I saw my family's spiritual life gradually disintegrate, my marriage end, and I was now struggling along in a midlevel nursing position as the single mother of four daughters.

I was trying to maintain a spiritual life for myself and the girls and felt that was all I would ever manage to do. I certainly wasn't qualified for more than that. And, besides, I was too old for the mission field, which I'd longed for earlier.

Then came that disturbing question: "What is that in your hand?"

OK, God, let's talk this out, I decided. Moses had an old stick. *What assets do I have?*

1. An old farmhouse on five acres, which I'm still paying off.
2. Two old junker cars so I have one to drive while they take turns at the repair shop.
3. A healthy body and a reasonably clear mind.

I determined that I did have as much as Moses did. At least God wasn't asking me to be responsible for half a million people.

Moses' old stick may not have seemed like much of anything, but look at what God did with it! He brought the plagues to Egypt. He changed the stick into a snake and back. He parted the Red Sea. He brought water out of the rock. He did all sorts of unexpected things. Maybe he could even find a use for some of the things I had.

That analysis was the beginning of my conscious decision to use the things I had for God, whether they were special or not. I figured God simply wanted me to use the materials he'd given me. He didn't want me to wait until I had everything matching, color coordinated, and scratch free.

So I set out on my great adventure—to let God do whatever he wanted with my "stuff."

First, I considered the cars. I had always used whichever car was working to offer rides to neighbors, take people to church, and chauffeur my children's classmates to Bible Club, Sunday school, and Pioneer girls. I couldn't think of anything else I could use the cars for.

Second, my healthy body was doing about all I could manage with my night-shift work plus taking care of the girls. My normally clear mind was barely holding its own.

That left my house to consider. It was roomy and old, but comfortable. It had its quirks. Nevertheless, we liked it and enjoyed having people over on Sunday afternoons. I hosted a weekly children's Bible Club and sometimes a women's Bible study. People seemed to feel at home there.

When the original owner had built the house, his family lived in the basement while he finished the two upper floors, so the basement was partially finished with a bathroom, kitchen facilities, and an outside entrance. Could the basement be turned into an apartment and set aside just for ministry? Was that supposed to be the "old stick" in my hand? My girls and I decided to put out some feelers.

I sold the wood-burning range that was downstairs and bought an electric stove and refrigerator, put a set of bunk beds in the small bedroom, moved in some more furniture, hung some bright yellow curtains, and gave the kitchen a fresh coat of paint.

Then I contacted the pastors of a dozen churches, explaining that I had a basement apartment available for anyone who might need something on a temporary or emergency basis. I explained that it was warm, safe, and clean, but not plush. It was to be used as a ministry apartment, and I would ask only enough rent to cover extra expenses.

Within a few weeks Carole, a teacher from a nearby school, called to tell me her husband had become violent. She and her six-year-old son needed a safe place to live. One of the pastors had told her about the apartment. She and her son moved in and stayed for a year, until she could get on her feet financially. We became very good friends.

That was only the beginning. The apartment was seldom empty for very long. Once, my friend Christi befriended a pregnant young woman at the Laundromat. This Christian woman had recently discovered that her husband was involved in crime, and she had slipped away from him with no place to go. Christi and I helped move her into the apartment that day. That night she asked me to take her to the hospital so she could deliver her baby. It was several more days before she and her new son actually spent their first night in her new apartment.

Once, a missionary family from Japan stayed for a short time. Another time, several young people who were living on their own for the first time used the apartment. Some of my residents were students at the local community college. One young woman became engaged while living with us. She married and moved away, and later the couple moved back with us for a short time while they saved for a down payment on their first home. One young family stayed there while the husband was in basic training with the air force. Another time an immigrant family from Ukraine stayed with us for three months.

During the ten years or so that the apartment was available, two or three dozen people lived there. Some, like Carole, stayed for a year or longer. Some stayed for only a week or so. Now, sixteen years later, I am still very close to some of those people. Only a couple of guests caused a problem, and when they did, the Lord always provided a creative solution and moved them out. Only once was anything stolen from me—and even then the items were later returned.

Eventually, I sold my five acres and moved away, and the house was torn down for a huge housing development much grander than my old farmhouse. So there's no longer even a trace of the old house. However, I have memories of faces and friendships that will last far beyond this life. My daughters learned the joys of having an open home and holding their possessions with an open palm. They still use their gifts of hospitality. I had no idea what God had in mind that day when he kept bringing that little question to my attention—"What's in your hand?"

— Merilyn Millikan

MEET THE CONTRIBUTORS

Anne Agovino is a mother and grandmother from St. Louis, Missouri. Her story is told by **Elsi Dodge,** a retired teacher who travels the continent in an RV, accompanied by her elderly beagle and a strange little cat. She volunteers in a Christian school, works with the youth at Boulder Chinese Baptist Church, and is a freelance writer. Her Web site is www.rvtourist.com.

Nancy J. Baker teaches College Writing at Nyack College. She and her husband teach Bible studies and lead small groups at their church. Her poems have been published in *Decision, War Cry,* and *Purpose* and her devotionals have appeared in the *Quiet Hour* and the *Secret Place.*

Sandi Banks is mom to six children and grandma to ten; she gave birth to her first book, *Anchors of Hope,* in 2002 (Broadman & Holman). Other published contributions include stories in *Reader's Digest* and the Kisses of Sunshine series (Zondervan).

Kimchi Lya Blow is a military spouse and mother of three. She currently lives in Savannah, Georgia, where she enjoys teaching and writing for her local church community.

Robin Caroll is the author of the Bayou series, available from Steeple Hill, Love Inspired Suspense, and is currently serving as president of American Christian Fiction Writers (ACFW). Robin's passion has always been to tell stories to entertain and uplift others. You can learn more about this Southern writer at www.robincaroll.com.

Jennifer Lynn Cary has written for pleasure for more than thirty years. She is a member of American Christian Fiction Writers, Romance Writers of America, and a CLASS graduate; her articles have been published in *The Inspirational Reader* newsletter, *Write to the Heart* and *Victory in Grace* magazines, and several compilations. Jennifer and her husband are now empty nesters in Arizona. You may check out her Web site at www.jenniferlynncary.com.

Katherine J. Crawford lives in Omaha, Nebraska, where she is a freelance writer. She enjoys playing chess, reading, and spending time with her husband of forty-eight years. Her Web site and e-mail addresses are www.katcrawford.com and lionheartedkat@cox.net.

Janey DeMeo is the founder of Orphans First (also "Sauver les Enfants"). She is married to Louis, the founder of one of the largest Bible institutes in France, where they lived as missionaries for twenty years. Janey has also mothered their two children and taught women. Currently she travels the world evangelizing and church planting, and she writes for various publications. Her book is *Heaven Help Me Raise These Children!* Learn more about her ministry at www.orphansfirst.org.

Midge DeSart is a wife, mother, and grandmother. Her book *Maintaining Balance in a Stress-Filled World,* published in 2003, is in its second printing. Besides writing, she is a church musician and a beading embellishment artist with many awards for her fiber art. She and her husband live in the Pacific Northwest.

Lisa Plowman Dolensky is the mom of three miracles and is celebrating twenty fulfilling years with her husband, Ed. Lisa, a UA graduate, continues nurturing others who are growing in God's garden as a 4K parochial preschool teacher and writer.

Beth Duewel lives in Ashland, Ohio, with her husband and three children. She is a regular contributor to *P31 Woman* magazine and a contributing author to *A Cup of Comfort Devotional for Women*. Catch more of her writing at www.bethduewel.com.

Connie Dunn believes in pursuing life passionately. She is a wife, mother, systems specialist, author, missionary, and aspiring life coach. She and her husband are empty nesters in Kansas City. Her Web site is www.spirit-led-coaching.com.

Liz Hoyt Eberle writes about everyday people who often do not see that God uses their struggles and joys to bless others' lives. The stories she weaves have been widely published. She loves hearing from readers at eberle2@hotmail.com.

Pamela Enderby just celebrated thirty-three years of marriage. She has five grown children and loves to read and write in her spare time. She finds her greatest joy in sharing her faith with others.

Sheila Farmer is a homemaker and freelance writer in Maryland, near Annapolis. She writes the community column for her local newspaper, the *Maryland Gazette.*

Suzanne Woods Fisher, who lives in California, is a contributing editor for *Christian Parenting Today* and has written for *ParentLife, Worldwide Challenge,* and *Marriage Partnership.* Her first novel, *Copper Star,* was recently published. Find Suzanne online at www.suzannewoodsfisher.com.

Evangeline Beals Gardner is a stay-at-home mom who teaches piano lessons and does freelance writing projects on the side. Her two daughters, ages eleven and eighteen, keep her household full of life, energy, and excitement. She enjoys being a praise and worship leader at her church and leading a Bible study in her home.

Sue Lowell Gallion is a freelance writer, currently focusing on inspirational writing and writing for children. She lives in the Kansas City area with her husband and two teenagers. She is a member of the Heart of America Christian Writers Network.

Sandra Glahn writes, teaches classes at Dallas Theological Seminary, and edits the seminary's magazine, *Kindred Spirit.*

Renee Gray-Wilburn is a writer in Colorado Springs and the stay-at-home mom of three children. She has numerous publications in both adult and children's markets.

Michelle Griep has been writing since first discovering Crayolas and blank wall space, and currently she is a frequent contributor to *devozine* and *Crosswalk.com.* When not working on the Great American Novel, she's a full-time, homeschooling mom with four children. She seeks to glorify God in all that she writes—except for that graffiti phase she went through as a teenager.

Mary A. Hake is a freelance writer and editor who has written hundreds of articles and contributed to a number of books. She enjoys writing children's stories and is working on a novel for teens.

Wanda Harpole, the owner of Heartland Lodge, told her story to **Patricia Lorenz,** an inspirational, art-of-living writer, speaker, and author of nine books. Patricia has had more than four hundred articles published in magazines and newspapers. She is also a contributing writer for many compilations and is an award-winning newspaper columnist.

Jennie Hilligus is an author from the Kansas City area who enjoys writing devotionals, fiction, nonfiction, and poetry. She and her husband have been married twenty-seven years and have two grown children and a son-in-law. Jennie spent fourteen years as a freelance artist for Hallmark Keepsakes.

C J Hines is a freelance writer living in Cedar Falls, Iowa. She is a former newspaper reporter and editor for a regional newspaper.

Lynn Ludwick, author, quilter, and mother of three, survived the ultimate empty nest and is now the grandmother of seven. She lives in a cute cottage with peach and orange walls, which she has dubbed the Peace Cottage.

Karen Mackey is a native of Wyoming and a self-described "prairie person." She is a lover of God and open spaces. In addition, she loves her husband, five children, and nine grandchildren. Karen has been a church secretary for twelve years and is a freelance writer.

Dana Mentink is a resident of California, where the weather is golden and the cheese is divine. After spending many years teaching elementary school children, she now writes fiction for the Wild Rose Press and Barbour Books. Her shorter pieces have appeared in several publications. She juggles her writing career with caring for a husband, two children, and a dog with social-anxiety problems. Visit her on the Web at www.danamentink.com.

Merilyn Millikan is a mom, a grandmother, and a great-grandmother who lives in Renton, Washington. At different points in her life, she was a full-time, stay-at-home mom; a full-time, working, single mom; and a full-time missionary. She is now retired and works part-time as a caregiver.

Karen Morerod is a freelance writer, speaker, and Bible study leader and lives contentedly in Kansas City, Kansas. She and her pastor-husband have three married children and two teenagers.

Jennifer Ochstein is a freelance writer living in northern Indiana. Though she's become used to the idea of being a "pink doily" at heart, she continues to try to break her pottery-painting addiction.

Barbara Oden is founder of Nevertheless Ministries, a devotional Web site for women. She enjoys reading, writing, and visiting her son who is away at college. Barbara is a teacher of single women at her church and enjoys an occasional quiet evening at home with Matilda, her dog.

Leslie J. Payne is a retired sign-language interpreter for the deaf. She and her husband, Richard, are grateful for every day of their married life. They live in Annapolis, Maryland, and enjoy family, travel, and sailing their boat, *New Life*.

Ellie Ray is a former kindergarten teacher who enjoys writing from her life experience.

Katy McKenna Raymond loves writing comedy about everyday family life. Someday, you may find her novels on the bookstore shelf; in the meantime, she blogs her funny business at www.fallible.com. Katy and her husband, Doug, enjoy an empty nest, where they frequently share Life Savors with their adorable adult kids.

Colleen L. Reece learned to read by kerosene lamplight and dreamed about someday writing a book. God expanded her dream: Five million copies of Colleen's 140 "books you can trust" have sold and are blessing readers.

Marilyn Rockett is wife to Chesley, mother to four sons, and "Mimi" to six grandchildren. She most recently authored *Homeschooling at the Speed of Life: Balancing Home, School, and Family in the Real World* (Broadman & Holman, 2007), and she is a seminar leader for homeschool and Christian women's groups. Visit her Web site at www.marilynrockett.com.

Carol Russell is a professional public speaker and an author. She and her husband, Bob, have been married for more than forty-five years and live in Fort Scott, Kansas. They have three daughters, five grandchildren, and one great-granddaughter.

Betsy Ann St. Amant, an inspirational writer in Louisiana with a B.A. in Christian Communications, has a heart for three things—chocolate, red polka-dot shoes, and sharing the amazing news of God's grace through her writing. Her first Christian fiction romance novel, *Midnight Angel,* is available on Amazon.com. Betsy enjoys reading, kickboxing, and writing.

Darlene Schacht has written more than one hundred humorous short stories, many of which have been published in local newspapers and online publications. She is the founder and editor of *Christian Women Online* magazine. She is also the author of the humorous devotional book *The Mom Complex: Discover the Woman God Designed You to Be.* Darlene and her husband, Michael, live in Manitoba, Canada, with their four children.

Lori Z. Scott has published more than four dozen devotionals, short stories, articles, puzzles, and poems for children, teens, and adults. The first two titles in her new children's chapter-book series came out in July 2007: *Meghan Rose on Stage* and *Meghan Rose Has Ants in Her Pants.* Her Web site is www.meghanroseseries.com.

Susan Stanley, a wife and a full-time mom by choice, is a former corporate consultant and current freelance writer. She writes during her children's naptimes and at night.

Rhonda Wheeler Stock has been a freelance writer for sixteen years. She was a humor columnist for *Today's Christian Woman* and has written articles and curriculum for other publishers. She and her husband live in Kansas and are the parents of three boys and a girl. Rhonda teaches junior high special education and enjoys prowling around flea markets, thrift stores, and antique shops.

Donna Collins Tinsley is a procrastinating, hormonally challenged, stay-at-home mom of four daughters (ages sixteen to forty) who aspires to write while homeschooling one daughter, dealing with stress, and chasing after a three-year-old grandson. She recently wrote a book called *Somebody's Daughter.* Donna is married to pastor Bill Tinsley. They live in Port Orange, Florida, where her goal is to minister to wounded women.

Paula Wiseman lives in Robinson, Illinois, with her husband, Jon, and children Lauren, Alan, and Rachel. She has written for children and teens and was a contributor to *A Cup of Comfort Devotional for Mothers.* She is currently working on a novel.

Jamie Speak Wooten is a writer, speaker, and Bible teacher. She creatively relates biblical truths to daily living through Speak for Christ Ministries and her monthly e-devotional for women entitled "Hey Girlfriend . . . It's Almost Friday!" She encourages women to truly experience God and his Word in their lives so they can understand God's purposes in their daily lives. E-mail her at speakforchrist@kc.rr.com to join her mailing list.

Arnita C. Wright is a wife, a mother, a short-story writer, and the author of two novels, *The Journey* and *The Stone.* Arnita conveys her love for God through powerful life messages. Please visit her at www.arnitacwright.org.

ABOUT THE AUTHORS

JAMES STUART BELL

James Stuart Bell is the owner of Whitestone Communications, a literary development agency. He consults with numerous publishers, represents various authors, and provides writing and editing services. He has previously served as executive editor at Moody Press, director of religious publishing at Doubleday, and publisher at Bridge Publishing. He coauthored the best-selling *Complete Idiot's Guide to the Bible* and numerous other Christian guides in that section for the Penguin Group. He has also contributed numerous Christian volumes to the best-selling Cup of Comfort series by Adams Media.

JEANETTE GARDNER LITTLETON

Jeanette Gardner Littleton, the author of about a dozen books including *When Your Teen Goes Astray: Help and Hope from Parents Who've Been There*, has thirty years' experience in the writing and editing fields. She has been on the editorial staff of eight publications, including *Moody Magazine*, and has written several thousand articles. A freelance writer and editor, she is content editor/consultant for several Christian publications, is a series editor for Barbour, and edits for other book publishers. Jeanette and her husband, Mark, share a passion for encouraging and equipping Christian writers as co-directors of Heart of America Christian Writers Network.

Our lives offer us . . .

- Delicious moments
- Salty moments
- Sour moments
- Bittersweet moments
- Warm moments
- Icy moments
- Exquisite moments

Live life more passionately—learn to savor
every moment, with more than ninety people
who have done just that!